Presented to:

_____

By:

_____

Date:

_____

QUIET MOMENTS
WITH GOD
FOR TEENS

HONOR
B O O K S

07 06 05 04 03   10 9 8 7 6 5 4 3 2 1

Quiet Moments with God for Teens
ISBN 1-56292-690-X
Copyright © 2003 by Honor Books
An Imprint of Cook Communications Ministries
P.O. Box 55388
Tulsa, Oklahoma 74155

INTRODUCTION

Life can get down right busy between school, friends, family, activities, and work. How do you make it slow down? Take a few quiet moments—for personal meditation, for fellowship with God. We need both in order to live balanced lives while meeting the complex demands we face every day.

As our world moves and swirls past us with great speed and intensity, it's tempting to put those quiet times aside and regard them as luxuries rather than necessities. But the truth is—moments of quiet tranquility are critical. They help us define our relationships, our roles, our priorities, and ourselves. Without them, we become slaves to our lifestyles rather than the masters of them.

We hope you will find that the devotions in this book help you make your quiet moments productive and inspiring. We have made them short enough to fit easily into your special time, yet long enough to provide a solid kick-off for your day. As you read, we hope that they will draw you closer to God.

RUNNING PERSISTENTLY

Bob Kempainen was determined to make the 1996 U.S. Men's Olympic marathon team. He was willing to go to any lengths, no matter how gut-wrenching.

On a hilly course in Charlotte, North Carolina, he won the trials—but was sick five times in the last two miles.

Kempainen, the American record-holder in the marathon, has experienced stomach troubles since junior high school. But that hasn't kept this medical student from pursuing marathoning.

It is God who arms me with strength and makes my way perfect. He makes my feet like the feet of a deer; he enables me to stand on the heights.

2 SAMUEL 22:33-34

"To stop was out of the question," he said, when asked about his physical condition. With the goal in sight, he knew there would be plenty of time to rest after the race and five months to prepare for the Olympics.

When God puts a desire in your heart to achieve a specific goal, you can have the confidence that He will give you the strength and the ability to accomplish it.

Every person has his or her own obstacles to overcome in life. In Kempainen's case, the condition of his stomach tried to hinder him from making the Olympic team. In your life it will be something else. But we all face difficulties and challenges on the road to success—and the difference between those who succeed and those who fail is simply persistence.

Life is not a level, smooth path but rather a series of hills and valleys. There are times spent on the mountain top, when everything seems clear and perfect. Then there are those times when we feel like we're wandering around in a dark cavern, feeling our way along and trusting God for every step of faith.

Take a moment and set your heart to be persistent in your faith—faith in God to lead you, pick you up when you have fallen, give you strength to go on, and ultimately bring you to victory.

Obstacles are those frightful
things you see when you
take your eyes off the goal.

HANNAH MORE

THROUGH THE MAZE

> We have this treasure in earthen
> vessels, that the excellence of the
> power may be of God and not of us.
>
> 2 CORINTHIANS 4:7 NKJV

Ihara Saikuku, the author of two enduring works,
The Japanese Family Storehouse and The Millionaire's
Gospel, had this to say about the challenges we all face
in the pursuit of personal success:

> To be born thus empty into this modern
> age, this mixture of good and ill, and yet to
> steer through life on an honest course to the
> splendors of success—this is a feat reserved for
> paragons of our kind, a task beyond the nature
> of the normal man.

Interestingly, Saikuku wrote this more than three
hundred years ago! He lived from 1642 to 1693. His
statement confirms the familiar axiom, "Nothing ever
changes." What was true about human nature three
hundred years ago is still true today.

Each one of us is born into what may be likened to a maze—with many options for false starts, unproductive detours, and dead ends. The person who makes wise choices and decisions is the one most likely to make it through the maze of life with greatest efficiency, ease, and productivity.

The analogy of a maze holds true for each day also. In any given day, we face numerous opportunities to make wrong turns or give in to temptation instead of taking that big leap of faith to continue in God's plan for our lives.

The Scriptures would agree with Saikuku that steering an honest course is "beyond the nature of the normal man." Rather than an attribute of the unusual or specially-gifted person, however, this ability to make good moral choices is regarded by the Scriptures as evidence of the Holy Spirit at work in a person's life. It is the Spirit who helps us choose good and refuse evil.

Whenever you are faced with a decision today, ask the Holy Spirit to guide you. Ask Him to show you the way through today's maze!

Before us a future all unknown,

a path untrod; Beside us a

friend well loved and known—

That friend is God.

ANONYMOUS

FAULTY ASSUMPTIONS

A traveler at an airport went into a lounge and bought a small package of cookies to eat while reading a newspaper. Gradually, she became aware of a rustling noise. Looking from behind her paper, she was flabbergasted to see a neatly dressed man helping himself to her cookies. Not wanting to make a scene, she leaned over and took a cookie herself.

The pride of thine heart hath deceived thee, thou that dwellest in the clefts of the rock, whose habitation is high; that saith in his heart, Who shall bring me down to the ground?

OBADIAH 1:3 KJV

A minute or two passed, and then she heard more rustling. He was helping himself to another cookie! By this time, they had come to the end of the package. She was angry but didn't dare allow herself to say anything. Then, as if to add insult to injury, the man broke the remaining cookie in two, pushed half across to her, ate the other half, and left.

Still fuming later when her flight was announced, the woman opened her handbag to get her ticket. To her shock and embarrassment, there was her pack of unopened cookies!

It's so easy to make assumptions about what is happening around us. We expect things to be a certain way based on past experience, what we know, or what we have been told about a situation. Assumptions are not always wrong, but they are never to be trusted. Too many times they lead to embarrassment and even destruction.

The Bible tells us that assumption is based on human reasoning and the driving force behind it is pride. As Obediah 1:3 says, it is pride—thinking we know everything—which allows us to be deceived.

Pride caused the woman in this story to assume she was right and the gentleman was wrong. Instead of seeing him through God's eyes and praying for wisdom to handle the situation God's way, she ignored the man. In the end, she was completely blind to his kindness toward her.

When you find yourself in a conflict with others, avoid prideful assumptions by walking in God's love. See other people and situations through His eyes. After all, your vision is limited, but He knows exactly what's going on!

> Pride is at the bottom
> of all great mistakes.
>
> JOHN RUSKIN

THE STILL, SMALL VOICE

In his book, Focus on the Family, Rolf Zettersten writes about his good friend, Edwin, who bought a new car. The car had lots of extra features—among them was a recording of a soft female voice, which gently reminded him if he had failed to fasten his seat belt or was running low on fuel. Appropriately, Edwin dubbed the voice "the little woman."

On one of his many road trips, "the little woman" began informing him that he needed to stop and fill his tank with gasoline. "Your fuel level is low," she cooed in her soft voice. Edwin nodded his head knowingly and thanked her with a smile. He decided, however, that he had enough gas to take him at least another fifty miles, so he kept on driving.

The problem was, in only a few minutes the little lady spoke the warning again—and again and again and again until Edwin was ready to scream. Even though he knew, logically, that the recording was simply repeating itself, it really seemed as though the little woman spoke more and more insistently each time.

My conscience is clear, but that does not make me innocent. It is the Lord who judges me.

1 CORINTHIANS 4:4

Finally, he'd had all he could take. He pulled to the side of the road and, after a quick search under the dashboard for the appropriate wires, gave them a good yank. So much for the little woman, he thought.

He was still feeling very smug for having had the last say when his car began missing and coughing. He had run out of gas! Somewhere inside the dashboard, he was almost certain he could hear the laughter of a woman!

Our manufacturer, God, has given us a factory-installed warning voice. It's called the conscience. Sometimes we may think it's a nuisance, overly insistent, or just plain wrong. However, most of us will learn sooner or later that it is often trying to tell us exactly what we need to know.

Whether you are being told to stop for gas or being warned not to turn off the main road, your conscience knows what is right. Follow it today, and see if you don't experience more peace about every decision you make.

> I will place within them as a guide My Umpire Conscience, whom if they will hear, Light after light well us'd they shall attain, And to the end persisting, safe arrive.
>
> JOHN MILTON

A LEATHER-BOUND COVER

Man looketh on the
outward appearance, but
the LORD looketh on the heart.

I Samuel 16:7 KJV

Dodie Gadient, a schoolteacher, decided to travel across America and see the sights she had taught about for the last thirteen years. Traveling alone in a truck, with her camper in tow, she launched out on her journey. One afternoon in California's rush-hour traffic, the water pump on her truck blew. She was tired, exasperated, and scared that in spite of the traffic jam she caused, no one seemed interested in helping.

Leaning up against the trailer, she finally prayed, "Please God, send me an angel—preferably one with mechanical experience." Within four minutes, a huge Harley drove up, ridden by an enormous man sporting long hair, a beard, and tattooed arms. With an incredible air of confidence, he jumped off and went to work on the truck. A little while later, he flagged down a larger truck, attached a tow chain to the frame of the disabled truck, and whisked the whole fifty-six-foot rig off the freeway onto a side street, where he calmly continued to work on the water pump.

The intimidated schoolteacher was too dumb-founded to talk—especially when she read the paralyzing words on the back of his leather jacket: "Hell's Angels—California." As he finished the task, she finally got up the courage to say, "Thanks so much," and carry on a brief conversation.

Noticing her surprise at the whole ordeal, he looked her straight in the eye and mumbled, "Don't judge a book by its cover. You may not know who you're talking to." With that he smiled, closed the hood of the truck, and straddled his Harley. With a wave, he was gone as fast as he had appeared.[1]

God has a way of opening our eyes, expanding our perspective, and showing us His greatest treasures—people—if we will look beyond our prejudices and preconceived notions. Be open to Him showing you a few of His treasures today!

Do not judge men by mere appearances; for the light laughter that bubbles on the lip often mantles over the depths of sadness, and the serious look may be the sober veil that covers a divine peace and joy.

EDWIN HUBBELL

THE TROUBLE WITH BEING RIGHT

Believe it or not, it's often harder to gracefully receive an apology than it is to issue one. As Christians, we know we are to forgive "seventy times seven" times (Matthew 18:22 KJV), but some of us can sincerely forgive and still project an air of superiority unbecoming to a child of the King.

> Take heed to your-selves: If thy brother trespass against thee, rebuke him; and if he repent, forgive him.
>
> LUKE 17:3 KJV

If you're waiting for someone to realize they owe you an apology, take some time to think of a response that reflects genuine forgiveness and allows the transgressor to feel he has retained your respect. Consider this humorous little story:

A passenger on a dining car looked over the luncheon menu. The list included both a chicken salad sandwich and a chicken sandwich. He decided on the chicken salad sandwich but absentmindedly wrote chicken sandwich on the order slip. When the waiter brought the chicken sandwich, the customer angrily protested.

Most waiters would have immediately picked up the order slip and shown the customer the mistake was his. This waiter didn't. Instead, expressing regret at the error, he picked up the chicken sandwich, returned to the kitchen, and a moment later placed a chicken salad sandwich in front of the customer.

While eating his sandwich, the customer picked up the order slip and saw that the mistake was his. When it came time to pay the check, the man apologized to the waiter and offered to pay for both sandwiches. The waiter's response was, "No, sir. That's perfectly all right. I'm just happy you've forgiven me for being right."

By taking the blame initially and allowing the passenger to discover his own mistake, the waiter accomplished several things: he allowed the passenger to retain his dignity, reminded him to be more cautious before blaming others, and created a better atmosphere for everyone in the dining car. Next time someone blames you for their mistake, don't get defensive, but find a creative way to make things right.

Forgiveness is a funny thing—it warms the heart and cools the sting.

WILLIAM ARTHUR WARD

CAN-DO ATTITUDE

Walter E. Isenhour wrote a clever poem that appeared in The Wesleyan Youth many years ago. Written for teens, its message is timeless.

Watch Your Can'ts and Cans

If you would have some worthwhile plans
You've got to watch your can'ts and cans;
You can't aim low and then rise high;
You can't succeed if you don't try;
You can't go wrong and come out right;
You can't love sin and walk in the light;
You can't throw time and means away
And live sublime from day to day.
You can be great if you'll be good
And do God's will as all men should;
You can ascend life's upward road,
Although you bear a heavy load;
You can be honest, truthful, clean,
By turning from the low and mean;

Jesus said unto him, No man, having put his hand to the plow, and looking back, is fit for the kingdom of God.

LUKE 9:62 KJV

18

You can uplift the souls of men
By words and deeds, or by your pen.
So watch your can'ts and watch your cans.
And watch your walks and watch your stands,
And watch the way you talk and act,
And do not take the false for fact;
And watch the things that mar or make;
For life is great to every man
Who lives to do the best he can.[2]

As your day progresses, keep in mind that your life goes in the direction you aim it. A popular saying in recent years sums up this idea succinctly: "Whether you think you can or can't—you're right." Have an "I can" attitude today, and then pursue excellence with all your ability.

People can alter their lives
by altering their attitudes.

WILLIAM JAMES

WHO'S WATCHING?

That ye would walk worthy
of God, who hath called you
unto his kingdom and glory.

1 THESSALONIANS 2:12 KJV

Even though we are Christians, we have to live our lives and conduct ourselves like everyone else, right? After all, we are only human!

Wrong! Once we have accepted Jesus into our lives, we have the supernatural power of the Holy Spirit to help us be and do more than what is humanly possible. Even nonbelievers know that people who call themselves followers of Christ should operate differently than those who don't.

Take, for instance, this account of a man named Roy. He had been a kidnapper and holdup man for twelve years, but while in prison he heard the Gospel and invited Jesus Christ into his life: "Jesus said to me, 'I will come and live in you, and we will serve this sentence together.' And we did."

Several years later he was paroled, and just before he went out, he was handed a two-page letter written by another prisoner, which said, "You know perfectly well that when I came into the jail, I despised preachers, the Bible, and anything that smacked of Christianity. I went to the Bible class and the preaching service because there wasn't anything else interesting to do.

"Then they told me you were saved, and I said, 'There's another fellow taking the Gospel road to get parole.' But, Roy, I've been watching you for two-and-a-half years. You didn't know it, but I watched you when you were in the yard exercising, when you were working in the shop, when you played, while we were all together at meals, on the way to our cells, and all over, and now I'm a Christian too, because I watched you. The Saviour [sic] who saved you has saved me. You never made a slip."

Roy says, "When I got that letter and read it through, I broke out in a cold sweat. Think of what it would have meant if I had slipped, even once."[3]

Who might be secretly watching you? A classmate, a sibling, a boss, or a family member who needs to know Jesus? You are His representative to those people.

A good example is
the best sermon.

SIR THOMAS FULLER

UNCHANGING HOPE

No one knows for sure when ships were first used for water transportation. The earliest evidence of sailing vessels dates from Egypt about the third millennium BC. Since then ships have changed considerably.

Today's passenger and cargo ships have no oars, sails, or masts. Modern vessels have all the conveniences of a great luxury hotel—gourmet cuisine, an array of entertainment, recreation, even swimming pools! One thing, however, has remained remarkably the same—the anchor. Except for the differing sizes, the anchor on Paul's ship of the first century and the anchor on the Queen Elizabeth II of the twentieth century are not much different.

> He will not fear evil tidings; his heart is steadfast, trusting in the LORD.
>
> PSALM 112:7 NASB

The same could be said of human life. Technology has brought staggering changes in virtually every arena of our lives. However people are still people. We experience the same struggles, temptations, joys, hopes, and sorrows of our ancestors—and our souls still need an anchor.

When Paul and his companions were shipwrecked on the coast of Malta, they dropped four anchors, which kept the ship from being dashed against the rocks. The writer of Hebrews tells us we have an anchor—our hope in Jesus Christ.

Jesus keeps us safe and secure in the midst of storms and uncertainties. No matter what we face, because He is Lord of our lives, we have hope—hope for the future, hope to be healed, hope to succeed, hope to be free, hope to help others.

Just as no experienced sailor would go out to sea without an anchor, we must never go anywhere without Jesus![4]

Hope is like the sun, which, as we journey toward it, casts the shadow of our burden behind us.

SAMUEL SMILES

TOY BOXES AND HEART GIFTS

Twenty large toy boxes lined the front of the auditorium—brightly painted and beautifully decorated. The lids were open with the names of children visible on the inside of each. As families came into the building, parents came forward with their children and placed gifts in the appropriate toy box. It wasn't long until every single toy box was filled to the brim.

The pastor stepped forward and began the morning service. The highlight of the service, though, was not the sermon; it was the choir from the children's home—yes, the very same children for whom the toy boxes were filled. They sang with transparent gratitude to the Father and an overpowering love for the Savior. This was their Christmas, and the small church in Austin, Texas, was their family.

Later that evening, Heather looked up at her father and asked, "Dad, do those kids really not have a mom or dad?"

"Yes, that's true," he replied.

> Inasmuch as ye have done it unto one of the least of these my brethren, ye have done it unto me.
>
> MATTHEW 25:40 KJV

"Well, then I feel good that we gave them presents, but won't they be sad without a mom and dad?"

"Sweetheart, I am sure that there are days in their lives when they are very sad. But I also know that they are very special to Jesus. And because of people like you and your brother, they know that they are loved."

"That's good!" she replied.

Without a doubt, this was one of the best Christmas gifts that could have ever been given to Heather and her brother Will, for they experienced the joy that comes from loving and giving as Jesus commanded.

What is a true gift? One for which nothing is expected in return.

CHINESE PROVERB

Such as I Have, I Give

Stir up the gift of God which is in you.

2 Timothy 1:6 NKJV

The word "talent" usually evokes images of great musicians, actors, and artists. When we think of talent in this limited sense, however, we feel untalented if we aren't gifted in any of these areas. The truth is, talents come in as many shapes and sizes as there are people, and God has given each of us one or more.

What are some of the not-so-obvious talents? Compassion is one. Do you feel kindness toward someone in a distressing situation? Then you have been given a talent! Use that feeling to write a letter of encouragement to someone you know who is in need. Do you like to plan surprises for people who may otherwise feel forgotten or left out? Then you are gifted! Don't bury that talent—use it to bring joy to another person.

Perhaps you have the gift of seeing something good in every individual. That is a gift all Christians need to cultivate. Affirm the good in someone, and then spread the "good news" about them. It usually takes someone else to see and bring out the best in people. You may see a talent in a person that he or she doesn't even know about!

Do you have a calm spirit in the midst of calamity? Can you think clearly when surrounded by turmoil? Then you are gifted—and your talent is very much in need.

That was a talent Jesus demonstrated when He slept through the storm on a boat, didn't lose sight of His purpose when facing the angry crowd, and faced His death sentence on the cross.

Do you have a cup of cold water to offer another person? Then you have a gift. Use it in the name of Jesus and for the glory of God.

Now think again. What talents do you have?

God does not require that each individual shall have capacity for everything.

RICHARD ROTHE

THE EMPTY TOMB

Philip was born with Down Syndrome. He was a happy child, but as he grew older he became increasingly aware that he was different from other children.

Philip went to Sunday school with kids his own age. The class had wonderful experiences together—learning, laughing, playing. But Philip remained an outsider.

As an Easter lesson, the Sunday-school teacher gave each student a large egg-shaped plastic container. Each child was to explore the church grounds and find something that symbolized new life to them, put it in their "egg," and bring it back to share with the class.

The group had a grand time searching the church yard for symbols. Then they gathered back in the classroom, put their eggs on the table, and watched with great anticipation as the teacher opened each egg. In one egg, there was a flower, in another a butterfly. The students responded with enthusiasm as the teacher revealed the contents of each egg—a branch, a leaf, a flower bud.

When the teacher opened the last egg, there was nothing in it. As could be expected, the class responded, "That's not fair—that's stupid! Somebody didn't do it right."

Philip went up to the teacher, tugged on her sleeve, and said, "It's mine. That egg is mine." The others laughed and said, "You never do anything right, Philip. There's nothing there."

Philip replied, "I did so do it. I did do it. It's empty—the tomb is empty!"

The classroom fell silent. From that day on, things were different. Philip became a full-fledged part of the class. They took him into their friendship. Philip had been freed from the tomb of his being different and was given a new life among his peers.[5]

Don't judge a tree by its bark.

FRENCH PROVERB

SOWING PEACE

The entire European continent felt the blows of hatred delivered by the evil tyrant Adolf Hitler. Millions of people died as a result of his platform of hate; millions more were scarred for life.

Heinz was an eleven-year-old Jewish boy who lived with his family in the Barvarian village of Furth during the 1930s. When Hitler's band of thugs came tearing through the village, Heinz's father lost his job as a schoolteacher. Recreational activities were forbidden, and Furth's streets became battlegrounds.

Neighborhoods were terrorized by the Hitler youth looking to make trouble. The young Heinz always kept alert to stay clear of them. When he saw them coming, he sought cover to get out of their way.

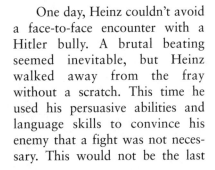

"Blessed are the peacemakers, for they shall be called sons of God."

MATTHEW 5:9 RSV

One day, Heinz couldn't avoid a face-to-face encounter with a Hitler bully. A brutal beating seemed inevitable, but Heinz walked away from the fray without a scratch. This time he used his persuasive abilities and language skills to convince his enemy that a fight was not necessary. This would not be the last time this young Jewish boy would use his peacemaking skills in Hitler-occupied Europe.

Eventually Heinz and his family escaped to safety in America, where Heinz would make his mark. He became known as a mediator and peacemaker among world leaders and nations. The young boy who grew up as Heinz anglicized his name when he came to America. We know him as Henry Kissinger.

Today, put your talents to use as a peacemaker and work together with those of different opinions. When you sow seeds of peace, you are doing God's work on earth, and you will reap a harvest of goodness.

First keep the peace within yourself, then you can also bring peace to others.

THOMAS Á. KEMPIS

LIVING BEYOND
THE THUNDER

Be strong and take heart,
all you who hope in the Lord.

PSALM 31:24

In The Diary of a Young Girl, Anne Frank wrote,
"I simply can't build up my hopes on a foundation con-
sisting of confusion, misery, and death."[6] She understood that hope originates somewhere beyond our
immediate circumstances. In fact, hope—real hope—
often stands alone in the darkness.

How was this young girl capable of courage and
faith far beyond her years? She refused to allow the
devastation of her times to shape her view of life. In
her words, "It's really a wonder that I haven't dropped
all my ideals. . . . Yet I keep them. I hear the ever-
approaching thunder. I can feel the sufferings of millions and yet, if I look up into the heavens, I think that
it will all come right."[7]

We can't know what horrors Anne Frank and her
family suffered during the Holocaust, but we do know

only her father emerged alive. Yet her words live on. Decades later, several generations have read and been touched by the diary of a young girl facing one of the darkest periods in world history—a girl who chose hope in the midst of hopelessness.

Life sometimes includes hardship. When tests come, we have the same choice Anne Frank had: hold on to our ideals or drop them. When life's circumstances sound like "approaching thunder," remember the simple truth in the life of a young Jewish girl. A foundation made of the right ingredients makes for an overcoming life. Holding tightly to one's ideals no matter the circumstance is a hallmark of character.

"In all things God works for the good of those who love him, who have been called according to his purpose" (Romans 8:28).

Hope not only bears up the mind under sufferings but makes her rejoice in them.

JOSEPH ADDISON

WAKE-UP CALL

Boot camp was a rude awakening for a young man who entered the Army to get away from his parents' rules. He reasoned that going into the service would give him the freedom to do whatever he pleased. He knew boot camp would be tough, but he was certain he could handle it. Besides, boot camp only lasted for six weeks. After that he would be free!

Upon waking that first morning to his sergeant's yells, the young soldier came face to face with the reality that Mom, Dad, and all his teachers clumped together couldn't compare to what he was about to face. His six weeks loomed as an eternity. He regularly wrote his family, and including the first thank-you notes his parents had ever received from their son. He even expressed thanks for what his teachers had done for him.

Awake to
righteousness,
and sin not.

1 Corinthians 15:34 KJV

This young soldier found out quickly the importance of learning how to handle what could attack a soldier in war. He was faced with a reason to wake up and a reason to be prepared. The sergeant trained the young recruits to anticipate the enemy's strategy, making certain they knew the enemy was lurking and ready to attack without warning. He taught them that the enemy is extremely cunning and watches and waits for the weakest, most vulnerable time to attack.

The Bible tells us to awake to righteousness and to prepare ourselves, so we will not sin. God has provided the right armor and training required to defeat the enemy. We become soldiers for Christ when we join His family. God's enemies are our enemies, and the battle is over the most precious of God's creations: the human soul.

God takes notice of clean hands,
not full hands.

LATIN PROVERB

LASTING LEGACIES

Marian Wright Edelman, attorney and founding president of the Children's Defense Fund, often speaks of how Martin Luther King had a profound impact on her life. All Americans have been affected by Dr. King's life in some way, and most have heard his famous comment, "I have a dream." But it was not his public persona that had an impact upon her; it was his willingness to admit his fears.

She writes, "I remember him as someone able to admit how often he was afraid and unsure about his next step. . . . It was his human vulnerability and his ability to rise above it that I most remember."

> Good will come to him who is generous and lends freely, who conducts his affairs with justice.
>

She should know about rising above fear and uncertainty because her life was not an easy one, and one wonders just how often she drew strength from the self-honesty and candor of Dr. King.

Ms. Edelman grew up during the days of segregation, one of five children, the daughter of a Baptist minister. She graduated from Spelman College and Yale University Law School and was the first black woman to pass the bar in the state of Mississippi. She is a prolific and gifted writer and has devoted her life to serving as an activist for disadvantaged Americans, especially children.

Hers is an incredible testimony to the belief in helping others to help themselves. She never doubted that she could make a difference. "I have always believed that I could help change the world because I have been lucky to have adults around me who did—in small and large ways."

We have the same opportunity. Will we respond as well as she? Will we help change the world?

> Charity is helping a man
> to help himself.
>
> MOSES MAIMONIDES

THE INVITATION

The son said unto him,
Father, I . . . am no more
worthy to be called thy son.

LUKE 15:21 KJV

Rita stood on the sidewalk, peering wistfully at the beautiful home. Through the curtained windows, she saw nicely dressed people chatting with one another and enjoying refreshments. In her hand she clutched an engraved, personal invitation to the dinner party. She had been invited to attend the evening's affair by her professor who was impressed with her academic abilities and wanted her to meet others at the university.

She carefully fingered the invitation, looked down at her nice "party dress," which seemed so dull and ordinary in comparison to the gowns she saw through the window, and with a sadness of the soul she turned and slowly walked away. Clutched between her fingers: the unused invitation.

This poignant and painful scene from the British movie Educating Rita demonstrates just how difficult it is for one to accept the possibility of a new life. Rita came from a lower middle class family, and no one in her family had attended a university before her. She struggled with feelings of inadequacy and was forever wondering how she would fit in. It is this sense of self-doubt that caused her to fail to take action on the invitation.

However, thanks to a persistent professor who saw more in her than she saw in herself, she eventually accepted his invitation to join a new world. By the movie's end, this once modest woman excels as a scholar.

The invitation to become and then excel as a Christian is for each of us. The greatest joy, though, is in knowing that our Master Teacher always sees much more in us than we usually see in ourselves.

God does not ask about our ability, but our availability. God wants us to be victors, not victims; to grow, not grovel; to soar, not sink; to overcome, not to be overwhelmed.

WILLIAM ARTHUR WARD

THE MAGIC OF INSTRUCTIONS

Angrily, the young man flung his wrench across the driveway and rolled away from the car. He had been trying for hours to change the brake pads on his small foreign car. It didn't help matters that he was at best a mediocre mechanic. Finally, in exasperation he stormed into the house and informed his father that something was seriously wrong with his car and he could not fix it.

"In fact," he shouted, "I don't know if anyone can fix it!"

His father quietly moved to the telephone, where he called his friend, a master mechanic. After he explained the situation, father and son ventured to the nearest library where they found a manual for the car. They carefully made copies of the pages giving directions on how to change the brake pads. Next, they stopped at a foreign-car auto-parts store and purchased a small but vital tool necessary for this particular job. Finally, they proceeded home to the car, and within thirty minutes the repair job was complete.

Pay attention and listen to the sayings of the wise.

PROVERBS 22:17

What made the difference? Three things: first, he contacted his father and then a master mechanic. The first instruction God gives us is to call upon Him. Second, they found the right set of instructions and carefully followed them. Sometimes, we insist on trying to do things without consulting the instructions. Finally, they secured the proper tool to do the job. God will always give us the right tool if we will go and secure it.

Whether we are talking about brake pads or critical life decisions, it is simply amazing—almost magical—how well things work out when we follow instructions.

A single conversation across the table with a wise man is worth a month's study of books.

AUTHOR UNKNOWN

THE GIFT OF FLIGHT

They call their flights "missions."

On any given day, the volunteers of AirLifeLine, a national nonprofit organization of recreational pilots, can be called into action to provide needy patients with transportation to distant hospitals for lifesaving surgeries and medical treatments. Without their assistance, many of the recipients, financially devastated by catastrophic illness, could not afford airfare to reach their medical facilities as quickly as needed.

You might not recognize these angels immediately. With members in all fifty states, the more than eight hundred AirLifeLine representatives come from every possible profession and walk of life.

> As each one has received a gift, minister it to one another, as good stewards of the manifold grace of God.
>
> 1 PETER 4:10 NKJV

But they share an irrepressible enthusiasm for flying and a desire to give something to their communities. These weekend pilots, always on the lookout for an opportunity to fly somewhere, are happy to donate their time, skills, and use of their aircraft to help those in need.

Their passengers are every bit as varied. The case could be a child in need of a kidney transplant or a cancer patient flying to a faraway research center for experimental treatment.

For Houston pilot Jed Goodall, "Every mission I fly is heartwarming. I just thank the good Lord that I can afford to fly an airplane. You get so much back yourself from doing this."[8]

What could be more rewarding than doing something you love and helping others at the same time? The Lord's gifts to us are bountiful, but they are multiplied when we take a talent He has given us and spread it around.

A generous action is
its own reward.

WILLIAM WALSH

THE LORD DIRECTS
MY STEPS

The mind of man plans his way,
but the LORD directs his steps.

PROVERBS 16:9 NASB

The birthday party was going well, and the thir-
teen-year-old girl was thrilled that all of her friends
could be there to celebrate with her. Each present was
"just what she wanted." The last game to play was Pin-
the-Tail-on-the-Donkey, and everyone was especially
excited because the winner would receive a ten-dollar
gift certificate for pizza. When the birthday girl had her
turn, she lost her footing and stumbled on top of several
of her friends.

It was very funny, but the girl wasn't able to get her
position right after that, and she continued to try to pin
the tail everywhere except near the game's paper donkey.
When the scarf was removed from her eyes and she saw
how far she was from where she needed to be, she said,
"I certainly needed someone to direct my steps."

God has promised to direct our steps if we will allow Him to do so. The plan for our lives was laid before the beginning of time. Each morning we can go to the Lord and have a fresh look at the direction He would have us go that day.

Are you faced with a major decision? Do you need direction and guidance? Throughout Scripture there are promises that God will show us the right path. We do not have to stumble or grope around blindfolded. Our Heavenly Father is eager to give us wisdom. All we need to do is ask, and He will direct every step we take.

I would rather walk with God in the dark than go alone in the light.

Mary Gardiner Brainard

DOUBLE BLESSING

British statesman and financier Cecil Rhodes, whose fortune acquired from diamond mining in Africa endowed the world-famous Rhodes Scholarships, was known as a stickler for correct dress—but not at the expense of someone else's feelings.

Once it was told that Rhodes invited a young man to an elegant dinner at his home. The guest had to travel a great distance by train and arrived in town only in time to go directly to Rhodes' home in his travel-stained clothes. Once there, he was distressed to find that dinner was ready to begin and the other guests were gathered in their finest evening clothes. But Rhodes was nowhere to be seen. Moments later, he appeared in a shabby old blue suit. The young man later learned that his host had been dressed in evening clothes but put on the old suit when he heard of his guest's embarrassment.[9]

Rabbi Samuel Holdenson captured the spirit behind Rhodes' gesture, saying:

> Kindness is the inability to remain at ease
> in the presence of another person who is ill at

In your godliness, brotherly kindness, and in your brotherly kindness, love.

2 PETER 1:7 NASB

ease, the inability to remain comfortable in the presence of another who is uncomfortable, the inability to have peace of mind when one's neighbor is troubled.

The simplest act of kindness not only affects the receiver in profound ways, but brings blessings to the giver as well. It makes us feel good to make others feel good. So do something nice for yourself today—commit a random act of kindness!

The greatest thing a man can do for his heavenly Father is to be kind to some of his other children.

HENRY DRUMMAND

MORNING THIRST

The need for a refreshing drink when we first wake in the morning is often so strong that we find ourselves anticipating the taste before we ever get a glass in our hands. That thirst is a driving force that nothing else will satisfy.

There is another thirst that needs to be quenched when we first wake up: a thirst we often ignore until it is so great, that everything else in our lives—relationships, our growth as children of God, our joy, our peace—begins to wither.

Patti did not have running water inside her home when she was a child. Not since then has she known that same level of satisfaction a morning drink of water can give. This was especially true if the water in the house ran out during the night when it was too cold or too stormy for anyone to make a trip to the source outside. Sometimes it was a long, long wait for morning.

My soul thirsts for God, for the living God.

PSALM 42:2 NASB

There is a source of living water that is available to us any time of the day or night. It never runs out, it never gets contaminated, it never freezes over, and it is always as refreshing throughout the day as it was with the first sip in the morning.

Renowned missionary Hudson Taylor said, "There is a living God, He has spoken in the Bible and He means what He says and He will do all that He has promised." He has promised to quench our thirst in such a way that we will never be thirsty again!

Are you anticipating a drink from God's cup of refreshing living water in the morning? God gives you permission to start sipping right now. Bon appetit!

> Every character has an inward spring; let Christ be that spring. Every action has a keynote; let Christ be that note to which your whole life is attuned.
>
> HENRY DRUMMOND

A WORK IN PROGRESS

We are His workmanship, created
in Christ Jesus for good works,
which God prepared beforehand
that we should walk in them.

EPHESIANS 2:10 NKJV

Many centuries ago, a young Greek artist named Timanthes studied under a respected tutor. After several years of effort, Timanthes painted an exquisite work of art. Unfortunately, he was so taken with his painting that he spent days gazing at it.

One morning, he arrived to find his work blotted out with paint. His teacher admitted destroying the painting, saying, "I did it for your own good. That painting was retarding your progress. Start again and see if you can do better." Timanthes took his teacher's advice and produced Sacrifice of Iphigenia, now regarded as one of the finest paintings of antiquity.[10]

Timanthes' teacher knew what many great artists know—we should never consider ourselves truly finished with our work.

When the legendary Pablo Casals reached his ninety-fifth year, a reporter asked, "Mr. Casals, you are ninety-five and the greatest cellist who ever lived. Why do you still practice six hours a day?" And Casals answered, "Because I think I'm making progress."

Maya Angelou applies that same logic to daily life. In her book, Wouldn't Take Nothin' for My Journey Now, she writes: "Many things continue to amaze me, even well into the sixth decade of my life. I'm startled or taken aback when people walk up to me and tell me they are Christians. My first response is the question 'Already?' It seems to me a lifelong endeavor to try to live the life of a Christian. . . . "[11]

How exciting it is to be a work in progress. With God's help, our possibilities are limitless!

What God does,
he does well.

JEAN DE LA FONTAINE

SUNRISE

Sunrise, shining its beams through the window on a cold winter's morning, is a welcome sight. Even if the air outside is icy cold, sunrise gives the illusion of warmth. With the rising sun, the city opens its shutters and makes preparations for the day; in the country, the farm animals are let out to pasture. You are off to school, Mom and Dad are on their way to work, and you each have a different perspective of the sunrise.

Sunrise happens whether we see it or not. Clouds may cover the sky so totally that we can't experience the beauty of the sunbeams making their way to the earth. No matter what the climate, the sun still rises in the eastern horizon and sets over the west. Sunrise is set by God's clock, and it is ours to enjoy in the early mornings when we can see it clearly. It is just as much there for us to enjoy when the cloud shadows cover it. We can trust it to be there—even though it may be hidden for a while.

> The sunrise from on high shall visit us, to shine upon those who sit in darkness.
>
> LUKE 1:78-79 NASB

We can also trust God to be there every morning because He is the one irrefutable reality in this life, and He remains constant and true!

Life is a mixture of sunshine and rain,
Laughter and teardrops,
pleasure and pain—
Low tides and high tides,
mountains and plains,
Triumphs, defeats and
losses and gains.
But there never was a cloud
That the Son didn't shine through
And there's nothing that's impossible
For Jesus Christ to do!

HELEN STEINER RICE

THE MASTER

The story is told of a concert appearance by the brilliant Polish composer and pianist Ignace Jan Paderewski. The event was staged in a great American music hall, where the artist was to perform for the social elite of the city.

Waiting in the audience for the concert to begin was a woman and her young son. After sitting for longer than his patience could stand, the youngster slipped away from his mother. He was fascinated by the beautiful Steinway piano awaiting the performance and made his way toward it. Before anyone knew what was happening, he crept onto the stage and climbed up on the piano stool to play a round of "Chopsticks."

The audience was horrified. What would the great Paderewski think? The murmurs quickly erupted into a roar of disapproval as the crowd demanded that the child be removed immediately.

Backstage, Paderewski heard the disruption and, discerning the

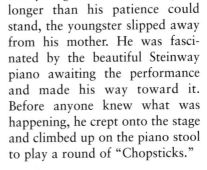

The LORD your God in your midst, the Mighty One, will save; He will rejoice over you with gladness, He will quiet you with His love, He will rejoice over you with singing.

ZEPHANIAH 3:17 NKJV

cause, raced out to join the child at the piano. He reached around him from behind and improvised his own countermelody to his young guest's "Chopsticks." As the impromptu duet continued, the master whispered in the child's ear, "Keep going. Don't quit, son . . . don't stop . . . don't stop."[12]

We may never play alongside a master pianist, but every day in our lives can be a duet with the Master. What joy it is to feel His love wrapped around us as He whispers, "Keep going . . . don't stop . . . I am with you."

I am the vase of God,
he fills me to the brim,
He is the ocean deep,
contained I am in him.

ANGELUS SILESIUS

BRAVEHEART

Beloved, thou doest a faithful work in
whatsoever thou doest toward them
that are brethren and strangers withal.

3 JOHN 1:5 ASV

Kevin tells the story of a dear friend, classmate, and church member who passed away suddenly.

At the funeral, people stood up one by one to tell stories about their friend, and soon a recurring theme emerged: that his single most outstanding trait was his willingness to serve others, no matter what the need. He was one of those people who was always ready to lend a hand—to run an errand, do odd jobs, or give someone a ride home. One of his friends mentioned how everywhere he went, he kept a toolbox in the trunk of his car, "just in case somebody needed something fixed."

More often than not, when we hear the word "courage," we think of heroic acts in times of crisis. But in our everyday lives, we shouldn't overlook the courageousness of simply being there. Lives are changed when we faithfully contribute to the good of our families, care for the elderly, or lend an ear to a troubled friend.

Persistence in making this world a better place to live—for ourselves and others—is definitely a form of courage.

Albert Schweitzer—the great Christian missionary, doctor, and theologian—was once asked in an interview to name the greatest living person. He immediately replied, "The greatest person in the world is some unknown individual who at this very moment has gone in love to help another."

As you go about your tasks today, remember that you could be someone else's hero.

A candle loses nothing by
lighting another candle.

AUTHOR UNKNOWN

FAITH IS A VERB

In You Can't Afford the Luxury of a Negative Thought, John Roger and Peter McWilliams offered a new description of faith. They chose the word "faithing" to describe their proactive approach to confidence in life's outcomes.

In their thinking, faithing works in the present, acknowledging that there is a purpose to everything and life is unfolding exactly as it should. It is actively trusting that God can handle our troubles and needs better than we can. All we must do is let them go, so that He can do His work.

> Faith is the assurance of things hoped for, the conviction of things not seen.
>
> HEBREWS 11:1 NASB

The Two Boxes

I have in my hands two boxes
Which God gave me to hold.

He said, "Put all your sorrows in the black,
And all your joys in the gold."

I heeded His words, and in the two boxes
Both my joys and sorrows I store,
But though the gold became heavier each day
The black was as light as before.

With curiosity, I opened the black.
I wanted to find out why
And I saw, in the base of the box, a hole
Which my sorrows had fallen out by.

I showed the hole to God, and mused aloud,
"I wonder where all my sorrows could be."
He smiled a gentle smile at me.
"My child, they're all here, with Me."

I asked, "God, why give me the boxes,
Why the gold, and the black with the hole?"
"My child, the gold is to count your blessings,
the black is for you to let go."[13]

Can a faith that does nothing be called sincere?

JEAN RACINE

PERFECT HARMONY

The late Leonard Bernstein—conductor, composer, teacher, and advocate—may well be the most important figure in American music of the twentieth century. With his personality and passion for his favorite subject, he inspired generations of new musicians and taught thousands that music should be an integral part of everyone's life.

As a public figure, Bernstein was larger-than-life—his charm and persuasiveness infectious. While his career progressed, he was constantly sought after for performances, lectures, and other appearances.

But it's said that in his later years, one way his personal life eroded was in his friendships. There came a time when he had few close friends. After his death, a comment from one of his longest acquaintances was that "You wanted to be his friend, but so many other people sought his attention that, eventually, the friendliest thing you could do was leave him alone."[14]

Scientific evidence now shows us how important friendships are,

A man who has friends must himself be friendly, but there is a friend who sticks closer than a brother.

PROVERBS 18:24 NKJV

not only to our emotional health, but our physical and mental health as well. But these most cherished relationships are a two-way street. A few tips for keeping friendships on track are:

Be aware of your friends' likes and dislikes. Remember your friends' birthdays. Take interest in your friends' hobbies. Become need sensitive. Keep in touch. Express what you like about your relationship with another person. Serve your friends in thoughtful, unexpected ways.[15]

Good friends are gifts from God. Is there someone you need to call today?

The only way to have
a friend is to be one.

RALPH WALDO EMERSON

A PHOTOGRAPHIC MEMORY

If we confess our sins, He is faithful
and just to forgive us our sins and to
cleanse us from all unrighteousness.

1 JOHN 1:9 NKJV

Famed photographer and conservationist Ansel Adams was known for his visionary photos of western landscapes, inspired by a boyhood trip to Yosemite National Park. His love of nature's raw perfection was apparent in his stark, mysterious black and white wilderness photos.

In 1944, he shot a beautiful scene, later entitled Winter Sunrise: The Sierra Nevada, from Lone Pine, California. It portrayed the craggy Sierra mountains in the bright morning sunlight, a small dark horse appearing in the foothills.

But the story is later told that, as Adams developed the negative, he noticed "LP" carved in the hillside. Apparently, some local high school teenagers had etched their initials on the mountain.

Intent on recapturing nature's original, he took a brush and ink and carefully removed the initials from his negative. The man who gave the Sierra Club its look believed in preserving, even perfecting nature, in life as well as in photography.[16]

Ansel Adams probably never gave a second thought to the unsightly scar on the mountain in his photo creation. In his mind's eye, he saw the beauty of the original and took steps to bring that beauty back into focus.

Someone once observed that "the purpose of the Cross is to repair the irreparable." Through the blood of Christ, we know that our sins have been forgiven—our scars erased—and that once removed, our sins are forgotten. The Lord remembers them no more. When we are willing to confess our sins, He takes joy in restoring us to our original beauty.

Forgiveness is the fragrance
that the flower leaves
on the heel of the one
who crushed it.

MARK TWAIN

GENTLE RIPPLES

Early in the morning a lake is usually very still—no animals, no people, no noise, no boats, no cars. All is quiet.

This is the best time to skip rocks. By taking a small, flat pebble and throwing it at the right angle, you can skip it across the water, leaving circles of ripples every time it makes contact with the lake. The ripples form small and very defined circles at first, then spread out and break apart until they vanish. If several people skip rocks at the same time, the ripples cross over one another and blend together to make miniwaves across the lake. The impact can be pretty amazing.

O God, thou art my God; early will I seek thee.

PSALM 63:1 KJV

For most of us, mornings are filled with so many things that need our attention that we find it difficult to spend time alone with God. However, the Lord set a marvelous example for us by rising early to listen to God. If we don't make time for this quiet morning time with God, we often find we don't have time during the day. Then we end up going to bed with regret or guilt. Maybe tomorrow, we think. But many times, tomorrow never comes.

When we spend time alone with God at the beginning of each day, we become acquainted with Him and start becoming like Him. Throughout our days, the ripple effect of our time with God in the early morning will impact the lives of those with whom we have contact.

When these ripples blend with others who spend time with God, we create miniwaves of love and joy. It all starts with a quiet time and a gentle ripple.

So here hath been dawning
another blue day;
Think wilt thou let it
slip useless away?

THOMAS CARLYLE

ENJOYMENT WITHOUT WINNING? YOU BET!

The two boys were acquaintances but not friends. In fact, you could easily consider them rivals. Steve was the stereotypical young athlete who was stronger, taller, faster, and better than most of his peers. Don was smaller and slower but filled with dogged determination and an intense desire to win. One evening during a Little League baseball game, a most remarkable event happened for the two young boys.

Steve had pitched a no-hitter the previous week, and his team was leading by one run at the bottom of the last inning when Don came up to bat. With runners on first and second base and two outs, Don needed to get a base hit for his team to win. The encounter was a challenging one with Steve nearly hitting Don with the first pitch. From that moment on, adrenaline surging, Don proceeded to swing mightily at the next three pitches—missing each one and striking out.

Shout for joy to the LORD.

PSALM 100:1

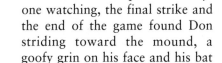

But to the surprise of everyone watching, the final strike and the end of the game found Don striding toward the mound, a goofy grin on his face and his bat forgotten in his left hand, with his right hand outstretched to shake hands with Steve. Steve came striding off the mound to meet him with his own hand outstretched and a small smile on his lips—not a smug grin of triumph, but a warm, delightful smile of a secret shared.

What happened? For just a moment, the joy of participating in the game superseded the need to win the game. Life can be like that, too. With the right approach, the joy of living can countermand the need to win, because we begin to trust God with the outcome while we enjoy the process.

Your living is determined not so much by what life brings to you as by the attitude you bring to life; not so much by what happens to you as by the way your mind looks at what happens.

Circumstances and situations do color life, but you have been given the mind to choose what the color shall be.

JOHN HOMER MILLER

Stay with Your Father

I am with you and will watch
over you wherever you go.

Genesis 28:15

Bobby was having the time of his life on the hiking trip. He, his father, two brothers, and uncle were all on a day hike to Blue Lake, four miles high into a wilderness area. The trail, as most mountain trails do, led upward by winding around and through tall pine trees. Occasionally, the trail would break out into small clearings and cross crystal-clear streams.

Bobby was determined to be the first person to the lake. The path was plainly marked and easy to follow, so he quickly pushed ahead of the small group. The sounds of the group's easy banter soon faded, and suddenly he found himself surrounded by stillness. He was alone. He was so far ahead of the group that he was out of sight and hearing distance.

The beautiful morning began to take on an ominous air. What if a bear were in the woods? What if some mountain man, gone crazy, were waiting with a hatchet in the trees? What if . . .

In a moment Bobby decided he would rather be with the group; he turned around and headed back down the path to meet them. In just a couple of minutes he was with them again. Safe!

Sometimes we get so anxious to be first that we run off ahead of everyone important to us. We can even get too far from God by relying on our own knowledge or expertise and place ourselves in dangerous circumstances. At that moment—and the moment will surely come when we realize how alone we are—we can always return to the safety of being with the Father.

God shall be my hope, my stay, my guide, and lantern to my feet.

WILLIAM SHAKESPEARE

GOD'S PROMISES

Our society is inundated with hundreds of reasons why being first is a goal to be obtained. It is necessary to be first in every line to get the best seat. Winning first place carries the most weight, the largest purse, and the most recognition. Rarely are we able to recall the second runner-up in any event. No doubt about it, first is the crème de la crème. Or is it?

> "Seek first His kingdom and His righteousness; and all these things will be added to you."
>
> MATTHEW 6:33 NASB

There is nothing wrong with obtaining first-place status. As a matter of fact, the Bible encourages us to set high goals and reach for them with perseverance. Each of us knows people we admire because of the goals they have set and reached through committed determination. But what about those who do their very best and never make the first string, never get the top grade, never win the trophy, etc.? What do they do with God's promises?

God has a plan for each of us. The stakes are often very high. The game plan will be interrupted many times by the devil. We will doubt, be discouraged, and face what seem to be impossibilities. However, God promises us that if we seek Him first, we have whatever we need—all of His blessings and all of His promises.

It takes faith! Some never make it to the finish line, yet their labor is rewarded because they did their best. The contributions of those on the sidelines or behind the scenes are rewarded, although not with a shiny plaque they can display.

Each of us can place first if we simply believe the promises of God and become dead to doubt, dumb to discouragement, and blind to impossibilities.

The great thing in the world is not so much where we stand, as in what direction we are moving.

OLIVER WENDELL HOLMES

CLUBFOOT

Phillip Carey, an orphan and the main character in the novel Of Human Bondage,[17] was born with what was once called a "clubfoot." Because of his deformity, his school classmates often made fun of him and excluded him from their boyhood games.

In one poignant scene, young Phillip is convinced that if he prays hard enough, God will heal his foot. He daydreams for hours about the reaction of his classmates when he returns to school with a new foot: he sees himself outrunning the swiftest boy in his class and takes great pleasure in the shocked amazement of his former tormentors. At last he goes to sleep knowing that when he awakes in the morning, his foot will be whole.

But the next day brings no change. He is still a clubfoot.

Although this is just one of many disappointments for young Phillip, this proves to be a pivotal point in his learning to cope with the harsh realities of his life. Drawing upon an inner strength he did not know he had, he found that his clubfoot would not determine his destiny. But how he responded to it would make all the

There was given to me a thorn in the flesh.

2 Corinthians 12:7 KJV

difference in his life. If he viewed it as a crippling deformity, he would live a limited life. Instead, he began to see his handicap as nothing more than an obstacle to be overcome, and it did not hold him back.

Life is filled with grand opportunities cleverly camouflaged as devastating disappointments. For Phillip Carey, it was a clubfoot. For the apostle Paul, it was a thorn in the flesh. Whatever it is in your life, don't despair. With God's help, you, too, can turn your scars into stars, your handicaps into strengths.

Obstacles in the pathway of the weak become stepping-stones in the pathway of the strong.

THOMAS CARLYLE

Make Me a Channel of Blessing

Since we have gifts that differ according
to the grace given to us, each of us
is to exercise them accordingly.

Romans 12:6 NASB

Can you imagine a professional football tackle pitching for a major-league baseball game? He might be able to throw the ball with speed because he is strong and in great physical condition, but he won't have a great knuckle ball or a split finger ball that just makes it over the inside corner of the plate for a strike. He isn't equipped to play that position in that setting.

While all athletes go through extensive training to strengthen their God-given talents, each player actually is a specialist in his or her sport of choice. There are rare occasions where an athlete can change from one sport to another and still play well. But even that athlete will function better in one particular sport, playing one particular position.

So, too, are our spiritual gifts. Each of us has talents, and God has asked us to be channels of blessing to others. We may be able to do many things—even do them well—but we will find the greatest fulfillment and success when we use our gifts the way God intended they be used.

Being prepared for the work God has called us to do begins with knowing what our gifts are, and then surrendering our gifts totally to Him. Knowing what we have to offer to our family, friends, and community helps us discover our unique place in God's plan.

Channels only, blessed Master,

But with all

Thy wondrous power

Flowing thro' us,

Thou canst use us

Ev-'ry day and ev-'ry hour.[18]

CLINGING VINES

Scuppernong vines are parasites that grow up the trunks of and cling to healthy, firmly rooted trees in the southern United States. This walnut sized, dark skinned wild grape is used to make jams and jellies, and some Southerners use the hull skins for cobbler pies. The fruit produced by these vines has served as an inexpensive treat to poor families in the South for many years. In recent years scuppernongs have become more popular and can be purchased at stores all over the South.

> "I am the vine, you are the branches; he who abides in Me, and I in him, he bears much fruit, for apart from Me you can do nothing."
>
> JOHN 15:5 NASB

As beautiful, diverse, and tasty as the scuppernong is, it cannot survive on its own. It needs the life support of well-established trees to cling to and draw its nourishment from. Should the scuppernong vine be pulled away from its host tree, it will dry up and stop producing fruit.

Like the scuppernong, we cannot survive without total dependency on God. Without Him, we have no true life source, no lifeline, no nourishment, and we cannot produce good fruit.

We can, however, learn to cling to the Lord by surrendering ourselves to Him. We can draw nourishment through Bible study, prayer, worship, service, and heartfelt obedience. Like the scuppernong, clinging to our Source will help us grow healthy and produce much good fruit.

All we want in Christ, we shall find in Christ. If we want little, we shall find little. If we want much, we shall find much; but if, in utter helplessness, we cast our all on Christ, he will be to us the whole treasury of God.

HENRY BENJAMIN WHIPPLE

DON'T BLAME THE LETTUCE!

One evening, several students spread Limburger cheese on the upper lip of a sleeping friend.

Upon awakening, the young man sniffed, looked around, and said, "This room stinks!"

He then walked into the hall and said, "This hall stinks!"

Stepping outside for some fresh air, he exclaimed, "The whole world stinks!"[19]

How long do you think it took for that sleepy student to discover the problem was right under his own nose?

It is easy, and maybe even our nature, to find fault with the outside world while remaining blind to the ways we contribute to the problem. Are there times when we're the problem?

When you plant lettuce, if it does not grow well, you don't blame the lettuce. You look for

> Now he who plants and he who waters are one; but each will receive his own reward according to his own labor.
>
> 1 CORINTHIANS 3:8 NASB

reasons it is not doing well. It may need fertilizer, or more water, or less sun. You never blame the lettuce. Yet if we have problems with our friends or our family, we blame the other person. But if we know how to take care of them, they will grow well, like the lettuce. Blaming has no positive effect at all, nor does trying to persuade using reason and argument.

In our relationships, it is our job to seek the most nurturing environment. We must avoid negativity and self-righteousness and protect our relationships from jealousy and anger. When we apply God's love and care to our dealings with the important people in our lives, our relationships will most certainly grow and flourish.

Sow a thought and you reap an act;
Sow an act and you reap a habit;
Sow a habit and you reap a character;
Sow a character and you
reap a destiny.

SAMUEL SMILES

GROW UP!

He will be like a tree firmly
planted by streams of water,
which yields its fruit in its season.

PSALM 1:3 NASB

"Grow up!" is a taunt often used by teenagers to their peers who, for whatever reason, aren't acting as mature as they should at the moment. The command is given with the attitude that the other person can simply make a choice to immediately grow up.

Commanding a friend to grow up doesn't do any more good than it would to tell a tree to grow up. There is a process that must take place, and that process takes time. Every living thing requires certain elements in order to grow—good soil, the appropriate amounts of sunshine and water, and plenty of time.

People, like trees, need a good start in order to be rooted securely. Young saplings can't mature into beautiful and tall shade trees without the right mixture of sun, water, rich soil, and space. As long as a tree is living, it never stops growing and never outgrows its need for nourishment. Most importantly, this process takes time—and lots of it.

In God's perfect timing, we will indeed "grow up." Like a baby taking the first steps, so we must be willing to let nature take its course. The growth process is a long one, and it is never really complete. Flourishing trees don't strain to grow. They merely follow the natural process God planted in them. And healthy trees don't decide to just ignore the nourishment of sun, rain, and soil. Instead, they continually draw life from these things.

No matter what our "season" of life, growing up is a continuous process—and it all happens in God's time.

Be not afraid of growing slowly, be afraid of standing still.

CHINESE PROVERB

CHILD'S PLAY

Professional golfer Tiger Woods is considered to be the top player in the world, with the potential to rank among the greatest of all time. Watching him line up a forty-foot downhill breaking putt, some may recall seeing him on the Tonight Show when he was about three years of age.

He was already showing a talent for the game, so a small putting surface was set up for him. A ball was placed in front of Tiger, about eight feet from the cup. He lined up the shot, putted, and missed.

Another ball was placed in the same position. He again prepared to putt—then picked up the ball, placed it six inches from the cup, and promptly sank the shot. Johnny Carson and the audience laughed and cheered to see a small child do what many adults would like to do. Of course, if he did that today, he would be ejected from the tournament.

A resident of a small town was once asked by a tourist: "Have any famous people been born here?" He replied, "No, only babies."

We all start out as "only babies," but our Creator has placed within us the greatest power in the universe: the ability to grow, day by day, as we respond to increasing challenges.

How will you meet your challenges today? You could grow more selfish, more reclusive, more pessimistic, or more filled with hate. Or, with the help of God, you can grow to be more understanding, optimistic, giving, and loving. You have been given this day to grow. Will you do it your way or His?

All growth that is not toward
God is growing to decay.

GEORGE MACDONALD

SONLIGHT IN MY GARDEN

The senior class project was to plant a memorial garden. Together the students tilled the soil, preparing it with the best additives, including peat moss, landscape mix, soil conditioners, and bark mulch.

The students disliked the flowers at the local nursery, so they begged their sponsor to let them order some unique varieties out of a mail order catalog. Carefully, they selected each one, often choosing the most expensive plants. They were confident theirs would be the best garden ever.

The tender plants arrived in the mail, and the students began working immediately. They planted and watered, fertilized, watched, and waited. But nothing happened. One by one, the leaves turned yellow and began to wilt. By the end of spring, not one plant remained. They all shriveled and died.

> Grow in the grace and knowledge of our Lord and Savior Jesus Christ.
>
> 2 PETER 3:18

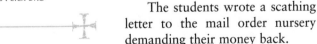

The students wrote a scathing letter to the mail order nursery demanding their money back.

Two weeks later, they received a reply.

"Students, your letter indicated you planted your flowers in a beautiful shady area and fed them the best nutrients possible. Your flowers failed to grow for the following reason: You planted them in the wrong place. You ordered flowers that must face the sun. Although you took great care to prepare the soil, without exception, these particular plants will die without sunlight. Next time, please read the directions before ordering your flowers and planting your garden."

Our lives are like that. We may spend great amounts of care and dollars to make ourselves beautiful. But if we are not facing the Son, we will wilt and eventually die. No amount of expensive "additives" will take the place of adequate Sonlight in our souls.

From morning to night keep Jesus in your heart, long for nothing, desire nothing, hope for nothing, but to have all that is within you changed into the spirit and temper of the Holy Jesus.

WILLIAM LAW

BLOOM WHERE YOU ARE TRANSPLANTED

You will be like a well-watered garden,
like a spring whose waters never fail.

ISAIAH 58:11

Kaylyn's family moved to a new city, far from family and friends. The movers arrived; the family unpacked their belongings, and her dad started his job the following week. Each day when he arrived home, his family greeted him at the door with a new complaint.

"It's so hot here."

"The neighbors are unfriendly."

"The house is too small."

"I don't have any friends here."

And each afternoon, he would listen to their gripes. "I'm sorry," he would say. "What can I do to help?"

Everyone would calm down, only to begin the same scenario the next afternoon.

One evening her dad walked through the front door with a beautiful flowering plant. He found a choice spot in the backyard and planted it. "OK," he said. "Every time you feel discontented, I want you to go and look at the garden. "Picture yourselves as that little flowering plant. And watch our garden grow."

Every week he brought home a new tree, flowering shrub, or rose bush for them to plant in the backyard. They cut some flowers from the growing plants and took them to a neighbor. Each morning they watered the garden and measured its progress. Friendships grew with other families on their block, and they asked them for gardening tips. Soon they were seeking spiritual advice as well.

By the end of the next year, the family's yard looked like a Better Homes & Gardens magazine feature.

Our Heavenly Father knows that we must all learn to bloom where we are transplanted. With His wise, loving touch, we will not only flourish, but we can produce the ever-blooming fruit of love, kindness, and contentment.

When life isn't the way you like it, like it the way it is.

JEWISH PROVERB

SMALL YET TALL

David was a shepherd boy who faced the fierce Philistine giant Goliath. His enormous opponent was armed and seemed to be well prepared to meet his enemy in battle. Goliath had seen many battles before. He was a warrior, but often he relied solely on his size and ferocity to win the battle before weapons were even drawn. He was the Philistines' icon of strength.

> In all these things we overwhelmingly conquer through Him who loved us.
>
> ROMANS 8:37 NASB

Mocking laughter could be heard all over the countryside when this powerful, tall, well-developed warrior stood there facing a boy. How could this be? Surely Goliath had the upper hand. He was the strongest and the best the Philistines had.

What did David bring to this battle? He was a boy, untrained in the weapons of warfare. He did not stand a chance. He was too young. For David's people, this seemed to be yet another disaster waiting to happen.

While Goliath mocked God, David worshipped the Lord. Goliath was smug in his sure victory; David asked God for a miracle. Goliath trusted his size and strength to save him; David relied on Someone far bigger and stronger. Though small, David trusted in a Mighty God. One tiny stone defeated the giant.

For thousands of years, tiny seeds planted in the cold, dark earth have yielded bumper crops of vegetation, towering trees, and every imaginable flowering plant. Faith plants a seed and looks for the harvest. David threw a stone and looked for a victory.

Our strength grows out of our weakness.

RALPH WALDO EMERSON

For the Least of These

In Henry Van Dyke's classic, The Other Wise Man, Artaban plans to join his three friends in Babylon as they followed the star in search of the King. He has three jewels to offer as gifts to the Christ Child.

But before he arrives, Artaban finds a feverish, poor Hebrew exile in the road. Torn between duty and desire, he ultimately stays and ministers for hours to the dying man. By the time Artaban arrives at the Bethlehem stable, the other Magi have left. A note encourages him to follow them through the desert.

> No one has ever seen God; but if we love one another, God lives in us and his love is made complete in us.
>
> 1 John 4:12

But Artaban has given the dying man his last provisions, so he returns to the city, sells one of his three jewels, and buys camels and food. In the deserted town of Bethlehem, a frightened woman cradling her baby tells Artaban that Joseph, Mary, and the Babe fled to Egypt to escape Herod's soldiers who are killing all the baby boys in the city. He offers a ruby to one of Herod's soldiers to save the woman's child.

Heartbroken that he has spent two of his gifts already, Artaban wanders for years seeking to worship the new King. He discovers no Baby King but finds many poor, sick, and hungry to feed, clothe, and comfort.

Many years later in Jerusalem, white-haired Artaban hears about a king being executed. He rushes toward Calvary to ransom the King with his last jewel. But instead, Artaban ends up rescuing a young woman from slavery.

At the end of the story, Artaban laments the turn of events. He wanted to bring gifts and minister to the King of Kings. Yet he spent his fortune helping people in need. The Lord comforts him with these words: "Verily I say unto you, inasmuch as ye have done it unto one of the least of these my breathren, ye have done it unto me" (Matthew 25:40 KJV).

Christmas is more than just a holiday to be celebrated once a year. And worship is more than mere words or gifts. Like the fourth wise man learned, real worship is a way of life.

> This is adoration: not a difficult religious exercise, but an attitude of the soul.
>
> EVELYN UNDERHILL

LIFE LESSONS

Speaking the truth in love.

EPHESIANS 4:15 KJV

"You know that what you did was wrong, don't you?"

The words echoed in Sandra's mind as she went home from school that evening. She was a good student who had never cheated in her life. Yet, this last assignment had been more than she could do. In a moment of desperation, she copied the work of another student.

Her teacher, Mrs. Wallace, had asked her to wait after class, and Sandra knew what was coming. Still, it was a shock when Mrs. Wallace asked her if it was really her work.

"Yes," she squeaked out, then wondered why she had lied.

Looking her straight in the eye, Mrs. Wallace carefully said, "You know that what you did was wrong, don't you? Take tonight to think about your answer, and I will ask you again in the morning if this is your work."

It was a long night for Sandra. She was a junior in high school with a well-deserved reputation for honesty and kindness. She had never cheated before, and now she had compounded her mistake by deliberately lying—and to someone she admired and loved. The next morning she was at Mrs. Wallace's classroom door long before school officially started, and she quietly confessed her misdeed. She received the appropriate consequences, a zero on the assignment and detention (her first and only detention).

Years later, Sandra often thought of that experience and felt gratitude for loving correction from someone she respected. Mrs. Wallace was willing to help Sandra make honest choices—even on the heels of making a dishonest one. For Sandra, this was a life lesson about taking responsibility for past mistakes and choosing honesty no matter what the consequences.

Power can do by
gentleness what violence
fails to accomplish.

LATIN PROVERB

How Firm a Foundation

The world's tallest tower stands in Toronto, Ontario, Canada. The first observation deck rises to 1,136 feet, and the second is even higher at 1,815 feet. Photographs and information located inside the tower help visitors comprehend the enormous undertaking of the project. Sixty-two tons of earth and shale were removed from fifty feet into the ground for laying the concrete that rises to the sky.

From 1972 to 1974, three thousand workers were at the tower site. Harnessed by safety ropes, some of the laborers dangled outside the giant for their finishing work. Remarkably, no one sustained injuries nor died on location.

Today a rapid elevator transports visitors upward for a breathtaking view of the city and all surrounding areas. Many say, "It was worth the money, time, and effort required to build the CN Tower."

"The rain came down, the streams rose, and the winds blew and beat against that house; yet it did not fall, because it had its foundation on the rock."

MATTHEW 7:25

We, too, need a good foundation for facing life each day. As we pray and spend time with our Heavenly Father, we are strengthening our spiritual foundation, our support base for life. We are able to see more from His point of view and not just our own. Thus we are not overwhelmed by whatever comes our way. When we feel we're hanging on the edge or suspended in midair, we can take courage in knowing He is holding us—firmly planted—in the palm of His hand. His foundation is strong and sure, and He will not crumble and fall.

When God is our strength, it is strength indeed; when our strength is our own, it is only weakness.

SAINT AUGUSTINE OF HIPPO

THE BEAUTY
OF DISCIPLINE

The ancient Chinese art of bonsai (pronounced bone-sigh) has existed as a horticultural art form for nearly 2000 years. The word "bonsai" literally means, in both the Chinese and Japanese languages, tree-in-a-pot. Practiced all over the world, bonsai is a sublime art where shape, harmony, proportion, and scale are all carefully balanced, and the human hand works in a common cause with nature.

A tree planted in a pot is not a bonsai until it has been pruned, shaped, and trained into the desired shape. Bonsai are kept small by careful control of the plant's growing conditions. Only branches that are important to the bonsai's overall design are allowed to remain, while unwanted growth is pruned away. The bonsai roots are confined to a pot and are periodically clipped.

The shape of these trees is always as found in nature. Some bonsai have been known to live for hundreds of years, and the appearance of old age is much

Blessed is the man you discipline, O LORD, the man you teach from your law.

PSALM 94:12

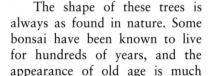

prized. The living bonsai will change through seasons and years, requiring pruning and training throughout its lifetime. And as time goes on, it will become more and more beautiful.

In truth, the bonsai would be nothing more than your average tree but for the discipline of the artist. Giving constant attention to the direction of growth, trimming away what is ugly or unnecessary, and strengthening the most vital branches result in a work of art that brings beauty to its surroundings for many years.

In our own lives, it is that same discipline that makes the difference between your average life and one that brings joy and beauty to its surroundings. With God's Word as our discipline, we, too, can become works of art.

Faith and obedience are bound up in the same bundle. He that obeys God, trusts God; and he that trusts God, obeys God.

CHARLES HADDON SPURGEON

BLACK MOUNTAIN

Many are the plans in a man's heart,
but it is the LORD's purpose that prevails.

PROVERBS 19:21

"**I** will just run away to Black Mountain!" screamed Richard.

"OK, if that's what you want, go ahead," responded his mother, opening the door and ushering him out to the front porch.

The silence descended on him like a cloak. The sun was long gone, and full night had settled upon the landscape. By the starlight he could just make out the dark form of Black Mountain to the north. Somewhere in the darkness, he heard the scurrying of a small animal and then the flap of wings in the night sky.

Suddenly, his heart was pounding in his chest, and his breath was coming quicker. Going to Black Mountain seemed like a really bad idea.

He thought, Why did I say that?

He sat on the porch with his knees drawn up to his chest and arms clasped around them. A tear trickled down his cheek as he tried to fight off his fears.

From the kitchen, he heard his father ask, "Richard, would you like to come to supper with the rest of us now?"

Sometimes when we get angry with ourselves, at others, at circumstances, or even at God, we want to run away. We stomp out our anger, and we make threats. We go out on the porch and pout. Yet, the Father waits patiently and even calls to us to rejoin the family. Love chases away fears, and restoration heals hurts.

O God, help us not to despise or oppose what we do not understand.

WILLIAM PENN

FINDING THE RIGHT "HOME"

A botanist, exiled from his homeland due to political unrest, took a job as a gardener in his new host country in order to support his family. His employer received a unique and rare plant from a friend. There were no care instructions with the plant, so the man put it in one of his hothouses, thinking it would do well there.

Only a few days had passed when he noticed the plant was dying. He called in his new gardener, the botanist, and asked if he had any ideas that might help to save the plant. The botanist immediately recognized this plant as an arctic variety that needed cold weather in order to survive. He took the plant outside in the frigid winter air and prepared the soil around it so the plant would gradually adjust to its new home. Almost immediately the plant went from wilting to vibrant.

Unaccustomed to the climate in the hothouse, the little plant must have felt the moisture draining from its small veins. The struggle to hold itself up to look the

> Those who wait for the LORD will gain new strength.
>
> ISAIAH 40:31 NASB

part of an expensive plant gave way under the weary load. The plant began to wilt and became only a shadow of its original beauty.

When the botanist rescued the plant and placed it in an environment suitable to its unique needs, the bowed-down foliage soaked in the nourishment and experienced renewal. Just like that rare plant, we can lose our spiritual strength if we live in an unhealthy environment. Seek God's help to find the right atmosphere for a joyous and productive life.

Attempt great things for God, expect great things from God.

WILLIAM CAREY

WHAT AM I KNOWN FOR?

"What does it matter what other people think of me? I don't care about them anyway!" Rebecca blurted out to her mom. "Why are you so concerned that I finish the service project in Girl Scouts? I'm gonna quit Scouts next year anyway, and besides I already have plenty of badges."

"Scouting and badges are not the issues," her mother replied. "I'm concerned with you and what you are known for. You are very caring and compassionate, warm and loving. You care deeply for the welfare of others. You made a commitment to the people at the assisted living facility, and many of them look forward to you visiting them. It's just hard for me to see you not keeping a promise."

"But I am tired of going up there every Saturday," Rebecca said.

Her mother suggested that they try to find a way to reduce some of her time commitment without abandoning the promise.

> Every tree is known by his own fruit. For of thorns men do not gather figs, nor of a bramble bush gather they grapes.
>
> LUKE 6:44 KJV

Before long, Rebecca felt hopeful again that she could complete the commitment without giving up all of her free time.

Later she commented to a friend that she hoped she would always live up to her mom's belief in her to be caring, compassionate, and trustworthy.

We are known more by what we do than by what we say. Sometimes commitments are overwhelming, particularly during the holidays or when pressures at school, home, church, or community seem to stretch us to the limit. Setting priorities and living by them—and most importantly, asking God for wisdom—will help us keep our promises without losing our hearts.

A good name is better than great riches.

MIGUEL DE CERVANTES

GARDEN VARIETY PLAYERS

Now you are the body of Christ,
and each one of you is a part of it.

1 CORINTHIANS 12:27

For years, Daron dreamed of playing basketball. He practiced daily after school.

His dad bought a backboard and goal, and together they shot hoops in the driveway.

In his freshman year of high school, Daron failed to make the basketball team. Discouraged, but refusing to quit, he kept practicing and attended all the games. He hung around after school and watched the guys practice. In his sophomore year, Daron tried out again. This time he made the team but sat on the bench most of the year. But he kept on practicing.

As a junior, Daron finally got his break and became a regular on the starting lineup. Although he could hit 75 percent of his shots, the coach rarely changed the rules: "Get the ball to Jim—as much as you can." Jim was the star of most games. He won the Most Valuable

Player award every year for three years and received a complete scholarship to a nearby college.

Daron expected no scholarship. After all, he was just a garden variety player. Then one day a coach from a prestigious university out of state called him, offering him a full scholarship.

"Why would you want me?" Daron asked.

"We've watched videos of you and your team in action, and we're impressed with your team skills. Lots of guys can be a star. But it takes a team—and a team player—to win successive games."

We may feel like "garden variety" Christians, being used in only small ways. We wonder how we could make a difference. But God is not in the business of recruiting "star" players. What He wants is a faithful heart, willing to serve Him as Heaven's team player.

The secret of success is to do all you can without thought of fame.

AUTHOR UNKNOWN

NOTHING IS IMPOSSIBLE WITH GOD

Scientists say it can't be done! It's impossible. Aerodynamic theory is crystal clear. Bumblebees cannot fly.

The reason is because the size, weight, and shape of the bumblebee's body in relation to the total wing spread makes it impossible to fly. The bumblebee is simply too heavy, too wide, and too large to fly with wings that small.

However, the bumblebee is ignorant of these scientific facts and goes ahead and flies anyway.

> I can do all things through Him who strengthens me.
>
> PHILIPPIANS 4:13 NASB

It was God who created the bumblebee and God who taught him how to fly. The bumblebee obviously didn't question God about the problem with aerodynamics. He simply flew. He didn't question whether God really knew what He was talking about. He simply flew. He didn't wonder if God really loved him when He gave him such small wings. He simply flew.

When God created us, He also equipped us for the life ahead. He says He knows the plans He has for our lives. Because He loves us, He has promised to be with us, to teach us, to carry us, to be our rock. All we have to do is trust and obey.

God is not limited by our understanding of how things happen. Just because we can't see something doesn't mean it's not real. Faith is, indeed, the substance of things not seen. Sometimes life is unexplainable, and the impossible happens. We can't always explain everything.

And just because we don't understand how something can be done, doesn't mean Almighty God can't do it.

When a man has no strength, if he leans on God, he becomes powerful.

DWIGHT LYMAN MOODY

Rise and Shine

Janie jolted awake at the sound of her alarm clock. This was her third day waking up in the middle of the night—at least it felt like the middle of the night even though it was actually early morning. She was not at all sure why she went through the trouble. It especially seemed vague and worthless the moments before her head settled back down onto the pillow.

"No!" She yelled at herself, waking up again with a start. She had promised she would do this, and she was going to, even if she went around for the rest of the day with a sleep-deprived, grumpy attitude. Janie stumbled to the bathroom, splashed some water on her face and carefully traversed the steps. Downstairs, she started a pot of coffee and sat down at the kitchen table. She had originally started doing her devotions on the sofa, only to discover they only lasted the five minutes it took for her to fall asleep again. At the kitchen table, she took out her Bible, her notebook, and a devotional. Her attitude brightened.

"Take my yoke upon you and learn from me, for I am gentle and humble in heart, and you will find rest for your souls."

Matthew 11:29

Once she was up, every moment was worth it. Meeting God in the early morning hours didn't make her grumpy as she always anticipated, but instead it revitalized her and brought her peace. The early morning moments gave her a chance to see the sunrise, to watch an occasional bird, to enjoy the silence of a world not yet awake. It took awhile to convince her body of the benefits of such early rising, but soon it became habit. After a while, the only time she experienced grumpiness was when she missed her morning meeting with God.

God's yoke is light; He is the rest for our souls that we think sleep should bring. Taking the time with our Savior in the early morning hours is better than fine cappuccino, the smell of omelets, and bacon. It is the best part of our day.

God is a tranquil being and abides in a tranquil eternity. So must your spirit become a tranquil and clear pool, wherein the serene light of God can be mirrored.

GERHARD TERSTEEGN

SACRIFICE AT SEA

"I am the living bread that came
down from heaven. If anyone eats
of this bread, he will live forever.
This bread is my flesh, which
I will give for the life of the world."

JOHN 6:51

Captain Eddie Rickenbacker, a famous World War I pilot, was forced down into the Pacific Ocean while on an inspection trip in 1942. The plane, a B-17, stayed afloat just long enough for all aboard to get out. Amazingly, Rickenbacker and his crew survived on rubber rafts for almost a month.

The men braved high seas, unpredictable weather, and the broiling sun. Night after night, they fought sleep as giant sharks rammed the rafts. But of all their enemies at sea, one was by far the worst—starvation.

After eight days at sea, all of their rations were gone or ruined by the salt water. They knew that in order to survive, they needed a miracle. According to Captain Eddie, his B-17 pilot conducted a worship service, and the crew ended it with a prayer for deliverance and a hymn of praise. Afterwards, in the oppressive heat, Rickenbacker pulled down his hat and went to sleep.

"Something landed on my head," said Rickenbacker. "I knew that it was a seagull. I don't know how I knew, I just knew." He caught the gull, which was uncharacteristically hundreds of miles from land. The gull, which seemed to offer itself as a sacrifice for the starving men, was something Captain Eddie never forgot.

In the winter of his years, every Friday evening at about sunset, Captain Eddie would fill a bucket with shrimp and feed the seagulls along the eastern Florida coast. The slightly bowed old man with the gnarled hands would feed the gulls, who seemed to come from nowhere. He would linger awhile on the broken pier, remembering a time when a seagull saved his life.

Jesus offered Himself as a sacrifice too. He is the Living Bread that came from Heaven. And just as Captain Eddie never forgot what one seagull meant to him, let's never forget what Christ did for us. Share the Bread of Life with those who are hungry.[20]

If Jesus Christ is God and died for me, then no sacrifice can be too great for me to make for him.

CHARLES THOMAS STUDD

THE EGG TEST

Have you ever tried to read a recipe while you were cracking an egg into a mixing bowl? If you have— and you're not very adept at it—you know it's not a pretty picture. If you don't keep your eyes on the egg, you'll end up with more egg on the counter than in the mixing bowl. Sometimes you may miss the bowl entirely, and the gooey egg makes a mess, running down the front of the kitchen cabinets, spilling onto the floor. Yuck! Any experienced cook will tell you that you'll have better success if you read the recipe first and then keep your eyes on the eggs.

> As the heavens are higher than the earth, so are my ways higher than your ways and my thoughts than your thoughts.
>
> ISAIAH 55:9

The Bible agrees. Well, maybe it doesn't talk about eggs and mixing bowls, but it does talk about our choices in life. When the Israelites first camped on the edge of the Promised Land, God instructed them to do some reconnaissance. Twelve men were sent to look the land over and report back to Moses with their findings. All twelve had seen God miraculously deliver them from slavery. All twelve had heard God's promise of protection. All twelve had experienced God's provision for their journey. But only two men remembered God and His faithfulness. Only two kept their focus on God; ten men were distracted by the sights and smells of Canaan. Ten men turned their eyes away from God and made a mess for the Israelites that took forty years to clean up. A glance away from God caused Israel's slippery slide to disobedience.

Whenever we focus on our problems instead of on God's promises and possibilities, we're in for a slippery slide too. The Bible says that God doesn't view things from our limited perspective. If we want the recipe of our lives to turn out for the best, we need to stay focused on Him. Let the egg test be your reminder: Whenever you crack an egg for a recipe, keep your eyes on the egg and remember to ask yourself if your heart is focused on God.

Great thoughts reduced to practice become great acts.

WILLIAM HAZLITT

BEAUTY FOR ASHES

Sitting at her round oak kitchen table, Sharon smiled as she sprayed the glass in the frame with glass cleaner. The words of the inspirational poem she had written for a friend, who was facing cancer surgery, came into sharp focus. Later, Sharon would take her "food for the soul" to her friend.

Looking outside, the gray December day reminded her of a similar day when she was in seventh grade. That day, the sky was laden with gray snow clouds ready to give the world a new birth. She could still see her teacher standing at the chalkboard, asking the class to write a poem.

Aware that Christmas was at the doorstep, she began writing. Her poem, so different from those of her classmates, was about the birth of the Christ Child. She took it home and rewrote it until the poem shone as though it were the star of Bethlehem itself.

"This is wonderful," the teacher said the next day. "Did you do this all by yourself?"

[He has sent me] to bestow on them a crown of beauty instead of ashes, the oil of gladness instead of mourning, and a garment of praise instead of a spirit of despair.

ISAIAH 61:3

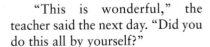

Beaming, Sharon said, "Yes, ma'am." Then the teacher read the poem to the entire class. She was beside herself with joy that day.

A couple of days later, however, the teacher asked to speak to her in the hall. There, after talking to another teacher, she accused the child of stealing the poem from a book. Brokenhearted, Sharon refused to write another poem—until twenty-five years later.

By then, Sharon was a woman who had returned to writing as a form of therapy during some difficult trials. One day, with Christmas again approaching, she wrote several Christmas poems. She sent them off to a publisher, expecting a rejection. Later, she received a letter indicating that two of her poems had been accepted.

Are you neglecting your talents because someone criticized you in the past? Don't let your gifts become ashes; turn them into a crown of beauty for God. Bless others with your talent! Whether it's cooking, serving, speaking, writing, or making something beautiful with your hands, do it for His glory.

Doubt is the hammer that breaks the windows clouded with human fancies and lets in the pure light.

GEORGE MACDONALD

VOICE FROM THE PAST

Faith by itself, if it is not accompanied by action, is dead. But someone will say, "You have faith; I have deeds." Show me your faith without deeds, and I will show you my faith by what I do.

JAMES 2:17-19

Laura was mixing cake batter when the phone rang. The voice on the other end said, "Hi. This is a voice from your past."

Since she didn't recognize the voice, Laura quipped, "Whose voice and from which past?"

Carrie had been in her ninth grade English class. She was an outstanding student, but very quiet. When Carrie's father took a job in another state, Laura lost contact with her.

Carrie bubbled with excitement. "I've been accepted at Harvard and start classes in the fall."

Laura listened intently. Was this the same Carrie who had needed lots of support from her friends? The same Carrie who had wrapped herself safely in a little shell?

To Laura's surprise, Carrie had changed. She was now taking control of her life and doing exciting things. She wasn't the least bit apprehensive about moving cross-country from her family to pursue her dreams.

As Carrie was closing the conversation, she said, "I wanted to make certain my good friends knew my dreams were finally coming true.

Laura's breath caught in her throat. She had never thought of herself as Carrie's good friend. Sure, she'd visited Carrie when she broke her arm, gone on class trips with her, and even eaten lunch with her in the school cafeteria, but she'd never thought of herself as Carrie's good friend.

How often do we touch someone's life with a random act of kindness? God uses ordinary people to make an extraordinary difference in the world around them. Find a way to be kind to another person today.

Can faith that does

nothing be sincere?

JEAN RACINE

A PERFECT RECIPE

A story is told about a young girl who attempted to bake her first cake from scratch. The finished product was inedible, and the girl sobbed her frustration to her mother. "I don't understand why it doesn't look like the picture," she cried.

"Did you follow the recipe?" asked her sympathetic mother.

"Yes," replied the girl. "I had to make a few substitutions, though. The recipe said to use baking powder, but I only had baking soda, so I used that instead. And I didn't have baker's chocolate, so I used a candy bar. And I only had half the amount of flour, so I substituted extra sugar to make up the difference. And then I was running late for class, so I took it out of the oven a few minutes early. Do you think it needed to bake for more than fifteen minutes?"

An angel of the Lord said to Philip, "Go south to the road—the desert road—that goes down from Jerusalem to Gaza." So he started out.

ACTS 8:26-27

What the girl failed to realize was the importance of following a recipe exactly as it is written. The proper oven temperature and time, and the exact amount of specific ingredients, blended in the right way, will yield a picture-perfect result. Anything less than complete adherence to a recipe invites disaster.

God has a recipe for each of our lives too. Our recipe will be a little bit different from another person's. One person may need more time in the oven to mature than someone else. One may need more sweet experiences in life. Another may need more of the oil of the Spirit to soften a hardened heart. And still another may need more sunny yolks to brighten a dreary existence.

Only God knows the best recipe for our lives. Ask Him today to show you what He wants you to add to the recipe of your life, what He wants you to do, and where He wants you to go. If you follow His recipe exactly, the results of your life can be just like the one He pictured for you.

All my requests are lost in one,
"Father, thy will be done!"

CHARLES WESLEY

THANK-YOU NOTES

Most books on etiquette include several pages about the topic of thank-you letters. Many people feel that a phone call expressing gratitude for a favor, gift, or invitation is enough thanks. But most of us really appreciate receiving a short note in our mailbox that says thank you. It may contain only a few sentences. It may be typewritten or scrawled by hand. But just knowing that someone took the time to write a word of thanks for something we said or did can leave a warm feeling in our hearts.

The person who receives the note is not the only one who is blessed. The one who sent the note benefits as well. When we take the time to sit down and collect our thoughts in order to put them on paper, we are actually taking time to dwell on the nature of the one who has done something for us. Quite often, because we have taken the time for that reflection, we find ourselves grateful for more than just one simple favor or gift.

The Bible says that we should be thankful to God "in all circumstances." We say thanks to God when we pray before meals. We often say thanks before we go to

Give thanks in all circumstances, for this is God's Will for you in Christ Jesus.

1 Thessalonians 5:18

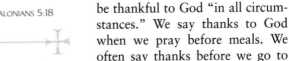

bed too. But why not be different today and write a thank-you note to God? Do you have a roof over your head? Do you have food to eat? Do you have friends and family who love you? Thank God for those things. Is the sun shining today? Is it the beginning or the end of the week?

When you finish your note, date it, sign it, and put it away in the back of your Bible or in a favorite book. You'll probably forget about it after a few days. But be assured that you'll find that note at an opportune moment, and you'll be reminded to say thank you again for the great things God has done for you.

We should spend as much time in thanking God for his benefits as we do in asking him for them.

VINCENT DE PAUL

Unwanted Invaders

See to it that no one misses the grace of God and that no bitter root grows up to cause trouble.

Hebrews 12:15

The Matthews' kitchen had been invaded. Not by ants or mice. Not by ravenous teenagers. But by moths. Just a few of them at first. But then, ten, fifteen, twenty a day. And not the big, fluttery kind of moths that hover around the porch light in summer. No, these were small, gray moths, barely a quarter of an inch long. Whenever someone opened a cupboard door, a moth inevitably flew out into the person's face. But where were they coming from? They had to find the hideout.

Systematically, the family began pulling open drawers and cupboards, finding small weblike nests that they washed away with disinfectant. After they had cleaned out all of the drawers and cupboards, the moth invasion slowed but never completely stopped. They could only assume that although they had wiped out some of the invaders' hideouts, there must be another stronghold somewhere.

With renewed determination, the family looked deeper for the source of the infestation, even checking behind the refrigerator and stove. But it wasn't until one of the kids saw a dead moth next to the dog's dish that they had their first real clue. They had recently purchased a new feeding system from a pet supply store, a container that held several pounds of dog food and distributed the food in measured servings into the dog's bowl. When they lifted the lid of the dog-food feeder and glanced inside, they knew they had finally found the source of the infestation and could once and for all get rid of the pests.

The Bible says that bad feelings can invade our lives like the moths invaded the Matthews' kitchen. An unkind word or action can become the catalyst for long-term bitterness between two people. Unless the root problem for those bad feelings is removed, the relationship may suffer severe damage. But if we take the time to talk through the misunderstandings, we'll reap the benefit of a strengthened relationship. Open communication in a relationship will help close the cracks of bitterness and rid us of the infestation of hard feelings.

The mind grows by what it feeds on.

JOSIAH GILBERT HOLLAND

SOMEONE WHO CARES

Maureen wearily put the box into the garbage can after binging on cold pizza. Her life had been difficult for months. As the rift in her parents' relationship continued to grow, her sense of security waned, and a fear of losing her family filled her heart. After a few months of a trial separation, her parents decided to finalize a divorce. It seemed that Maureen couldn't shake the ever-increasing gloom that grew heavier by the day.

At first her friends asked if there was anything they could do. Others made sure she was included in plans to go to the mall or to see a movie. But after a few weeks, no one asked how she was doing anymore; her friends had gotten on with their lives and figured Maureen had gotten used to living in a single-parent household. But she had not gotten used to it. A deep sorrow had settled in upon her heart, and joy seemed unattainable.

One day when her father dropped her off from their weekly visit, she stopped by the

> "When you give to the needy, do not let your left hand know what your right hand is doing, so that your giving may be in secret. Then your Father, who sees what is done in secret, will reward you."
>
> MATTHEW 6:3-4

mailbox on her way to the door. A small "thinking of you" card was tucked inside. It was signed, "Someone who cares." A ray of sunshine touched her heart as she read those simple words.

Someone really cares, she thought. She didn't know who it was, but she knew that someone was concerned about the situation that overshadowed her life. All day long she wondered who had been so kind. She looked at the card over and over, trying to see if she could recognize the signature. She knew that the person was praying for her, and she wanted to let her know how much she appreciated it.

As the weeks and months passed, Maureen continued to receive greeting cards from this anonymous person. The signature was always the same. But no one ever confessed to being the sender. Only God knew who uplifted her spirit. And for the sender, that was enough.

When you give, take to yourself
no credit for generosity unless
you deny yourself something
in order that you may give.

SIR HENRY TAYLOR

Spiritual Physics

"Michael!" Maury's voice carried through the quiet house.

"Yes, Maury?"

"Michael! Come bounce me!"

Michael looked out the window to the trampoline that seemed to take up half the yard. With a smile he grasped his little brother's hand and went out to bounce him. It was an odd sort of pride he took in being able to skyrocket his little body into the air. He outweighed him by a number of pounds, and his weight caused him to go higher than any of his friends could take him. It was just a simple matter of physics, really; the heavier your partner, the higher you go.

It's no different spiritually. The people you surround yourself with will either send you skyrocketing into spiritual understanding and maturity or leave you grounded and struggling.

He who walks with the wise grows wise.

Proverbs 13:20

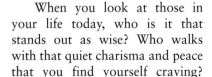

When you look at those in your life today, who is it that stands out as wise? Who walks with that quiet charisma and peace that you find yourself craving?

What would it take to call that person? Keep it simple and comfortable. Sit together at lunch, grab a slice of pizza after school, or simply spend an afternoon talking. Or perhaps you can find an activity you both enjoy. Surround yourself with people who will encourage your growth.

The Bible says in James 1:5, "If any of you lacks wisdom, he should ask God." Ask God to expand your wisdom and your world.

To seek wisdom in old age is like a mark in the sand; to seek wisdom in youth is like an inscription on stone.

SOLOMON BEN GABIROL

WRONG ROUTE

Wait for the LORD; be strong and take
heart and wait for the LORD.

PSALM 27:14

Downtown Seattle, sitting in the hotel lobby and waiting for a bus. Lizzy and Karen had broken free of a conference and were ready to explore the city that surrounded them. They'd been waiting for the bus for twenty minutes and found themselves impatient and eager. There was so much to do—so much to see!

Moments later, a bus pulled up. "It's not the one they said we should take," Lizzy said, smiling as she began walking toward the doors, "but it's headed in the same direction! Let's go!" They climbed on board—two Midwestern girls, heading for the sights. As the bus made its way through the dark and scary underbelly of the city, the girls huddled together in a small corner of the bus. The driver seemed amused by their predicament, and their fellow passengers seemed anything but willing to help them find their desired destination. They grasped each other's hands and tried to look less like tourists and more like residents. That only served to emphasize their discomfort.

Lizzy and Karen ended up staying on the bus for the whole route. Arriving back at the hotel, they were slightly shaken and had only lost a little time. They grinned at each other ruefully and waited, and waited, and waited for the right bus.

Is there a bus you're tempted to climb aboard because you're tired of waiting? Is there a relationship, a direction you're thinking of taking that may not be God's best for you? There is much to be gained by waiting in the lobby for the right bus. God will not abandon you in your search. He is there, ready and waiting with His answer, reminding you of His sovereign will and His ability to take you where you need to go. It's OK to wait on Him. In fact, it's much safer and a whole lot wiser, especially when you consider the alternative.

All comes at the proper time to him who knows how to wait.

SAINT VINCENT DE PAUL

Second Impressions

Was that the doorbell? Peggy peered through a crack in the living room draperies. She hardly knew her new neighbors, but she could see that the lady from across the street stood impatiently on the front porch. Peggy barely had time to open the door before the neighbor blurted out, "Neighborhood caroling. Saturday night. Meet at our house—7:00 P.M." Without giving Peggy a chance to reply, the neighbor hurried back across the street.

Though the neighborhood looks friendly with all of its Christmas decorations, the people sure aren't, thought Peggy. The elderly man next door only grumped at her whenever she said hello. And the weird couple behind her house kept a toilet on their front porch. Strange!

You are to judge your neighbor fairly.

Leviticus 19:15 NASB

When Peggy heard the sounds of caroling that frosty Saturday evening, something prompted her to bundle herself into her coat. As the neighbors caroled from house to house, Peggy tagged along, singing and listening to conversations. What she heard surprised her. The "impatient" neighbor lady took care of a handicapped son who required round-the-clock supervision. The "grumpy" neighbor had a speech impediment that made his words come out in grunts and growls. The "weird" man with the toilet used his unusual porch decoration as a unique conversation starter to tell others about God's love. The more Peggy heard, the more she realized that her first impressions of her neighbors had been wrong.

Later, as the neighbors gathered around steaming mugs of cocoa, Peggy decided to make some "second" impressions. She smiled at the "impatient" neighbor and said, "Hi, I'm Peggy. Do you have a minute to talk?"

Don't judge anyone harshly until you yourself have been through his experiences.

JOHANN WOLFGANG VON GOETHE

BETTER THINGS IN MIND

"**Y**ou just don't want me to have any fun!" Dell slammed out of the house and stomped through the backyard. He had no idea where he was going and no way to get rid of his anger, and he was a little nervous that he might be acting childish.

Dell hated the control his parents exercised over him. His friends got to do whatever they wanted, and no one cared. They could stay out late and watch whatever movies they wanted, and some of them were dating already. At fourteen, Dell felt he should have the same privileges. What made those other kids so special? Why didn't his parents trust him?

"Dell?" It was his dad. For a moment, Dell was tempted to ignore him, but he couldn't find the resolve. He turned around reluctantly.

> The LORD disciplines those he loves, as a father the son he delights in.
>
> PROVERBS 3:12

"What?" he asked. He almost missed the football flying through the air and had to quickly throw up his hands to block it. "Geez, Dad!"

He held the pigskin in his hands, tempted to toss it aside. But there was his father, waiting patiently, a smile on his face. Dell swallowed his anger and tossed the ball back. He supposed there could be worse things than having a father who tossed a football around with him, a dad who wanted to keep him pure of heart so that he would do what was right.

How often do you find yourself storming away from God's presence, holding on to something that He has asked you to let go of? How often do you resist His authority because of what your friends are doing? We need to keep in mind that the Father who corrects us knows where we are headed. He wants to keep our vision unclouded so He can lead us to the life He has set aside for us. Allow God's correction to be the greatest affirmation of His love and hope for your life.

Look upon your chastenings as God's chariots sent to carry your soul into the high places of spiritual achievement.

HANNAH WHITHALL SMITH

Guilty Snacking

"Watch and pray so that you will
not fall into temptation. The spirit
is willing, but the body is weak."

MARK 14:38

Stacie was sitting in the classroom when she first heard the commotion.

"No way!"

"Check it out!"

"Who's got some quarters?"

Stacie got up from her desk and walked cautiously toward the sound of money and elation. She rounded the corner to discover three of her friends gathered around the vending machine. They were inserting change, picking out items, and receiving both the snack and their money back. The machine had a loose wire and was giving out free food.

Stacie grinned. No breakfast that morning and quarters in her pocket made for a happy young woman. She pushed her way through the crowd and gave it a try. Three quarters . . . some powdered donuts. Three quarters back . . . a big cinnamon roll. Three quarters back . . . a bag of chips. Carrying her quarters and her unexpected breakfast, she headed back to her desk with a smile on her face.

It wasn't until she sat down that the guilt (and the calories) settled heavily on her conscience. It wasn't right! No matter that everyone else seemed to be OK with it. No matter that the vending machine guy was always grumpy and never stocked the items she liked . . . no matter about any of that! This was wrong. It was stealing, and she couldn't do it.

Oh, but how her stomach growled! Surely it would be OK if she had one bite . . . just one.

Stacie ate it all. But when the vendor came later, she dug into her pocket and paid for all three items. Her friends looked at her oddly, but she felt much better.

Sometimes it's easier to ignore the little things that no one else cares about—to join others who believe that if no one knows, it can't possibly hurt. Today, take a stand for the little acts of truth—the small steps of honesty and courage. Though some may mock you, you just may earn the respect of others, and God will use that to draw them to His heart.

'Tis one thing to be tempted,

Another thing to fall.

WILLIAM SHAKESPEARE

THE HAND OF FRIENDSHIP

It's not always easy to love. Growing up, Ben and Mary constantly fought. As brother and sister, they were inseparable, but they were interested only in tormenting each other—a push here, a shove there, stolen cookies, disappearing toys.

One spring afternoon, their mother reached her limit. She sat down both of her children and looked from one to the other. "I've had enough of your fighting. For the rest of the day, I don't want to hear a single raised voice, a thud from hitting one another, a scream, or a cry. I want you to love each other and be kind. Period. End of story. Just do it." She got up, brushed herself off, and went back to her tasks, unable to do or say any more.

> "This is my command: Love each other."
>
> JOHN 15:17

Ben and Mary sat and looked at each other. Love each other? How could they love each other? Just by being told? Especially when the sight of the other was enough to bring mud bombs and hair-pulling to mind? But they had never seen their mother quite so angry.

A few moments passed in silence, until Ben finally reached out and took Mary's hand. "Want to go to the mall?"

Mary smiled and said, "OK."

Of course, it's not always quite as easy as grabbing someone's hand and going shopping, but it's not as hard as we might think. Sometimes loving each other is simply a matter of letting go, starting anew with a fresh page before you, and deciding that the past is gone and that all you have is the future to mold. It's a matter of extending your hand in friendship and choosing to play rather than argue.

God commands us to love one another. Can you think of someone you have refused to love? Is there something you can do to extend a hand of friendship? Even if it is rejected, God asks only that you do your part. He will see to the rest. You never know; it may work out better than you imagine. They might even say, "OK!"

> They are the true disciples of
> Christ, not who know most,
> but who love most.
>
> FREDERICH SPANHEIM THE ELDER

THE GOD WHO NEVER SLEEPS

In March of 1975, a tornado raked an eight-mile path across Atlanta, Georgia, snapping pine trees like so many toothpicks. Civil defense officials estimated the damage to be as high as thirty million dollars.

Even today, Gloria remembers that day as though it were yesterday. She was a college freshman then and had worked part-time as a secretary at a small office. The office was closed that Monday so they could do some remodeling.

That morning as Gloria got ready for class, she noticed the sky outside turn an ominous black. The wind picked up, and trees bowed like rubber. She watched metal garbage cans being tossed down the street. Then the driving rain hit. The last thing on Gloria's mind, though, was a tornado.

> Cast all your anxiety on him because he cares for you.
>
> 1 Peter 5:7

After a quick trip to the library, she drove home. Visibility was poor as the rain slanted in sheets across the road. When she passed by her office, she almost wished she had gone to work, so she wouldn't have to battle the weather all the way home. The constant scraping of the windshield wipers grated on her nerves, so she turned on the radio to drown out the sound. The news reports were unbelievable! A tornado had been spotted in the Atlanta area. She accelerated, urging her car toward home.

Not until later did she learn that the tornadoes that whipped through Atlanta had destroyed the building where she worked. When she finally went back to the office and surveyed the damage, she found everything in shambles. She trembled when she saw the collapsed concrete wall on top of her desk and shuddered to think what might have happened had she gone to work.

What a blessing to know that God is omnipresent! He is the One who neither slumbers nor sleeps. He promises to be with us and deliver us even in the midst of a whirlwind. Look to God when darkness blankets your world, and He will show you the way home!

The wise man in the storm prays to God, not for safety from danger, but for deliverance from fear. It is the storm within that endangers him, not the storm without.

RALPH WALDO EMERSON

DESTINED TO WIN

Carry each other's burdens, and in this
way you will fulfill the law of Christ.

GALATIANS 6:2

Anne-Marie could feel the stitch in her side as she drew each ragged breath. Ten more strides, now five, now two. She held her arm out and handed the baton to the runner waiting in front of her. "Go, go, go!" she yelled. Her friend, Misha, took the baton and began to run. Her pace was quick and her prospects good, if only because she was refreshed and ready to run. Anne-Marie bent over and filled her lungs in great gasps. She could not have run another step. Thank goodness, Misha had been ready.

That's what teamwork is all about. As lovers of God, we carry the weight of responsibility to be there for our friends. We hand off to one another the care and love of our Father. When one is weary, the other is strong; when one is disheartened, the other believes. That's the way God designed the system to work. We're not supposed to run our races alone!

Sheryl experienced this firsthand. After a bout of illness in her family, her church and small Bible study group had taken turns visiting and bringing her family dinner. Now they had the opportunity to do the same as God blessed them with health and healing.

Like a well-trained, cross-country running team, we need to be refreshed and ready to run when the baton is handed our way. Yet we also need to be willing to receive when we can't walk on our own. Loving and caring for one another is the light by which we see our God. It's the best "warm fuzzy" in the world to know His love so intimately.

Is there someone you can love today? Someone who may need a card, a thought, a prayer? Or are you the one with the stitch in your side, ready to receive? In either case, allow yourself to reach out and be a part of the team that God has put together. We're destined to win!

Teach me to feel another's woe, To hide the fault I see; That mercy I to others show, That mercy show to me.

ALEXANDER POPE

LIGHT AND FLUFFY

"What's that?" the little girl asked, as she watched her big sister carefully mix the ingredients for bread.

"Yeast," her sister replied. "That's what makes the bread rise. We have to cover the dough with a cloth and put it in a warm place if we want our rolls to be light and fluffy."

"What shall I compare the kingdom of God to? It is like yeast that a woman took and mixed into a large amount of flour until it worked all through the dough."

LUKE 13:20-21

Not fully understanding the way yeast works, Mary was impatient. She continued to lift the cloth in order to see the round balls of dough that sat in the baking dish. After a while, she realized that they were growing larger.

Finally, they placed the rolls in the preheated oven. Mary watched through the glass window as the tops began turning golden brown. The scent permeated the whole house. When the rolls were done, Mary was allowed to brush a small amount of butter on the top of each one.

Mary's big sister thought about the look of amazement on her little sister's face when she saw how the bread had doubled in size. Her faith, she realized, was a lot like that dough. The more she prayed and studied God's Word, the larger her faith grew. And just as the rolls needed to remain warm in order to rise, she needed to keep her heart warm in order to serve God and others.

Today, keep a warm smile on your lips and a glow in your eyes. With a "light and fluffy" attitude toward life, we can rise up in the midst of trouble and show others the warmth that only God can provide.

The world is a looking-glass and gives back to every man the reflection of his own face. Frown at it, and it in turn will look sourly at you; laugh at it, and with it, and it is a jolly, kind companion.

WILLIAM MAKEPEACE THACKERAY

THE TATTERED BIBLE

Sarah's worn and tattered cookbook sat on a desk in the corner of the kitchen. Some of its pages were stuck together with drops of cake batter or cookie dough. Practically every page was stained, but it was obvious which recipes were her favorites. Those pages were barely readable. Between the leaves of the book were recipes from newspapers and store packages that she had carefully cut out over the years.

Sarah couldn't get along in the kitchen without her trusted cookbook. Not only did it provide a list of ingredients needed and instructions for preparing her favorite dishes, it provided many useful facts to enable her to run her kitchen efficiently.

Let the Word of Christ dwell in you richly as you teach and admonish one another with all wisdom.

COLOSSIANS 3:16

"Learning to read a recipe correctly is the most important part of cooking," she told her daughter many times.

Sitting close beside that trusted cookbook was the Bible. Like the cookbook, its pages were worn. It held clippings of memorable events that had taken place in her life and the lives of her family members over the years. Ink spots dotted the pages of her favorite Scripture passages. After many years of use, certain verses were difficult to read.

"Learning to understand the Bible and using it as a guideline for life is the most important part of living," she told her daughter. "This is God's instruction book designed especially for us. Everything that you will ever need to know about life is written on these pages."

By her example, Sarah taught her daughter that a used Bible is the most valuable tool for living. She sought God's guidance through His Word on a regular basis. Not only had it provided her with security and hope, it also helped her to live a life pleasing to Him.

That tattered Bible explained a lot about Sarah's life. All the ingredients and instructions were there; she only needed to follow them in order to find the strength, wisdom, and courage that characterized her life.

Wisdom is oftentimes nearer when we stoop than when we soar.

WILLIAM WORDSWORTH

TODAY'S SURE THING

The steps of a good man are
ordered by the LORD.

PSALM 37:23 NKJV

In his book, The Chance World, Henry Drummond describes a place in which nothing is predictable. The sun may rise, or it may not. The sun might suddenly appear at any hour, or the moon might rise instead of the sun. When children are born in Drummond's fantasy world, they might have one head or a dozen heads, and their head or heads may not be positioned between their shoulders.

If one jumps into the air in the "chance world," it is impossible to predict whether the person will ever come down again. That he came down yesterday is no guarantee he will come down the next time. Gravity and all the other natural laws change from hour to hour.

Today, a child's body might be so light it is impossible for her to descend from a chair to the floor. Tomorrow, the child might descend with such force, she falls through all three levels of a three-story house and lands near the center of the earth.

In the final analysis, The Chance World is a frightening world. While most people enjoy a certain amount of spontaneity in their lives, they enjoy life more when it is lived against a backdrop of predictability, surety, and trustworthiness.

The Scriptures promise us that the Lord changes not. He is the same yesterday, today, and forever (Hebrews 13:8). Furthermore, His natural laws do not change unless He authorizes their change for the good of His people. His commandments do not change. His promises to us are sure promises. We can know with certainty, "The steps of a good man are ordered by the Lord."

The Lord may have some surprises for you today. They are a part of His ongoing creation in your life. But His surprises are always custom-designed for you on the rock-solid foundation of His love. It is always His desire that you experience the highest and best in your life. You can count on Him!

All but God is changing
day by day.

CHARLES KINGSLEY

Do Your Best

Do you ever feel inadequate? Unworthy? Most of us do from time to time. And we all know people whom we think are too successful to have those same feelings.

Martin Luther, the sixteenth-century German preacher and Bible scholar who initiated the Protestant Reformation, sounds like the type of man who would be eminently sure of himself. Any man who would dare to publicly question the theology of his church—in a time when it could have cost him his life—could not be a man who had doubts about himself. Or could he?

> It will come about that whoever calls on the name of the LORD will be delivered.
>
> JOEL 2:32 NASB

In truth, Luther spent his early years obsessed by his presumed unworthiness. He periodically fasted and mistreated his body in an attempt to "earn" God's favor. On a pilgrimage to Rome, he climbed the Steps of Pilate on his knees, kissing each step. He wrote later that in those years he was constantly confessing his sins to God, yet he never felt he had done enough.

One day while reading the book of Romans, Luther realized he could not earn his salvation. The Bible says we receive salvation, we do not earn it (Romans 4:13-14).

Those verses of Scripture liberated Luther, radically changing his opinion that his works made him worthy of God's grace.

Luther recognized Jesus Christ had already done all the "earning" necessary for his salvation. He simply needed to receive what Jesus had done—that He had paid the price for his sin on the cross—by faith.

On days when we fall flat on our faces in failure or just feel low, we need to remind ourselves that our mistakes are not the end of the world. Our inadequacy is not our doom. Our salvation doesn't depend on how well we manage to color inside the lines!

Perfection may be our aim, but when we realize we haven't arrived there, we need to relax and turn to the Lord, saying, "Forgive me for what I have done, and for what I have left undone. I trust You to be my Savior, my Deliverer, my Hope, and my Perfection." He is and He always will be!

The farther a man knows himself to be from perfection, the nearer he is to it!

GERARD GROOTE

THE MORNING SACRIFICE

The Levites were never given the option to skip morning devotions. They were commanded to keep the morning sacrifice every day, without exception. As part of the morning ritual in the Temple, the high priest had these three duties:

1. to trim the lamps, making sure each oil cup of the menorah had sufficient oil and that the wicks were properly positioned,
2. to burn sweet incense on the incense altar,
3. and to burn the fat of the "peace" offerings.

Once a week, as part of the morning ritual, the priest replaced the "shewbread" that was on constant display before the Lord.

The priest performed these functions in silent worship, wearing a highly symbolic vestment. As he worked, the only sound was the light tinkling of the bells on the hem of his garment.

Their duty was . . . to stand every morning to thank and praise the LORD.

1 CHRONICLES 23:28, 30 NKJV

This ancient ritual may seem strange and of little meaning to us today, but one great lesson we can draw from it is this: the morning sacrifice involved all of the senses and the mind. The priest stood before the Lord with his identity clearly displayed; he stood before the Lord for examination.

His sacrifices touched upon all aspects of his humanity: the lamps symbolized his need for light—the ability to see with spiritual eyes. The incense was a picture of his need to dwell in an atmosphere infused with God's holy presence. The peace offerings were a sign of his need for peace with God and his fellow man. And the "shewbread" demonstrated his need for daily provision, which only the Lord could provide.

This was a ceremony that, in its silence, spoke clearly: "We need You. Without You, we have no life, no wholeness, no meaning."

We may not have a ritual to follow in our morning devotional times, but we must come before the Lord with the same spirit of dependency and obedience. The day ahead of us is not ours. Our lives belong to God (1 Corinthians 6:20).

Everything we need, He will supply. The day is His, even as we are His.

For anything worth having one must pay the price; and the price is always work, patience, love, self-sacrifice—no paper currency, no promises to pay, but the gold of real service.

JOHN BURROUGHS

MORNING PEOPLE

God called the light Day, and
the darkness He called Night.

GENESIS 1:5 NKJV

God made both the day and the night, and He
called both of them good. It seems God also made
"morning people," who have their greatest energy level
in the morning, and "night people," who are most productive in the late hours. Let's look at some of the joys
of being a morning person.

God promised the children of Israel they would see
the glory of the Lord in the morning (Exodus 16:7). This
promise came to them when they were hungry and in
need of bread to eat. God supplied manna every
morning until they reached the promised land. Like the
children of Israel, we too can see the glory of the Lord
when we seek Him in His Word. Each morning He provides the nourishment we need for the day.

Another blessing of morning time is it often brings
an end to suffering and sadness (Psalm 30:5). Each day
brings us a new opportunity to seek God for a fresh perspective on the problems and needs in our lives. When
we give every minute and every circumstance of each

day to the Lord, we can expect to see His light dawning throughout our day.

There are many examples in Scripture about people who rose early to meet God or to be about doing God's will, among them Abraham, Moses, Joshua, Gideon, Job, and even Jesus. The Gospels tell us that Jesus went at dawn to teach the people who gathered in the temple courts.

The most glorious event of Christianity—the Resurrection—occurred in the early morning. Each morning we can celebrate Jesus' Resurrection as we watch the light of the day dispel the darkness of night.

Make it the first morning business of your life to understand some part of the Bible clearly, and make it your daily business to obey it in all that you do understand.

JOHN RUSKIN

No Darkness Here!

Once upon a time a Cave lived under the ground, as caves have the habit of doing. It had spent its lifetime in darkness.

One day it heard a voice calling to it, "Come up into the light; come and see the sunshine."

> The path of the just is like the shining sun, that shines ever brighter unto the perfect day.
>
> PROVERBS 4:18 NKJV

But the Cave retorted, "I don't know what you mean. There isn't anything but darkness." Finally the Cave was convinced to venture forth. He was amazed to see light everywhere and not a speck of darkness anywhere. He felt oddly warm and happy.

Turnabout was fair play and so, looking up to the Sun, the Cave said, "Come with me and see the darkness."

The Sun asked, "What is darkness?"

The Cave replied, "Come and see!"

One day the Sun accepted the invitation. As it entered the Cave it said, "Now show me your darkness." But there was no darkness!

The apostle John opens his Gospel account by describing Jesus as the Word and as the Light—"the true light that gives light to every man" (John 1:9). It is John who also records Jesus proclaiming, "I am the light of the world. Whoever follows me will never walk in darkness, but will have the light of life" (John 8:12).

Jesus made this statement at the close of a feast, just as giant candelabra were being extinguished throughout the city of Jerusalem. During the feast these lamps had illuminated the city so that night seemed to be turned to day. "My light is not extinguishable," Jesus was saying, "regardless of the times or seasons."

As this day begins, remember that you take the Light of the World with you wherever you go; and regardless of what may happen during your day, His light cannot be put out.

Light is above us, and color around us; but if we have not light and color in our eyes, we shall not perceive them outside us.

JOHANN WOLFGANG VON GOETHE

TRUE VALUE

In the J. M. Barrie play, The Admirable Crichton, the earl of Loam, his family, and several friends are ship-wrecked on a desert island. These nobles were adept at chattering senselessly, playing bridge, and scorning poorer people. However, they could not build an outdoor fire, clean fish, or cook food—the very skills they needed to survive.

Stranded on a desert island, what the earl's family and friends did know was entirely useless for their survival. Had it not been for their resourceful butler, Crichton, they would have starved to death. He was the only one who possessed the basic skills to sustain life.

In a great turnabout, Crichton became the group's chief executive officer. He taught the earl and his family and friends the skills they needed and organized their efforts to ensure their survival until their rescue.

"The last will be first, and the first will be last."

MATTHEW 20:16

It is always good to remind ourselves of our "relative" place in society. If we are on top, we need to remember we can soon be at the bottom. If we perceive ourselves as at the bottom, we need to know that in God's order we are among "the first."

In The Finishing Touch, Chuck Swindoll raises the issue of perceived significance by asking about the people behind these Christian greats:

Who taught Martin Luther his theology and inspired his translation of the New Testament?

Who visited with Dwight L. Moody at a shoe store and spoke to him about Christ?

Who was the elderly woman who prayed faithfully for Billy Graham for over twenty years?

Who found the Dead Sea Scrolls?

Who discipled George Mueller and snatched him from a sinful lifestyle?[21]

We may not achieve the fame and recognition from people that we would like to have in this life, but God doesn't call us to be well known or admired. He calls us to be faithful to Him in whatever situation we find ourselves. When we are, we can see more clearly when He promotes us and gives us favor with others.

> He who knows himself
> best esteems himself least.
>
> HENRY GEORGE BOHN

ON THE ROAD AGAIN

God did not give us a spirit of
timidity, but a spirit of power,
of love, and of self-discipline.

2 TIMOTHY 1:7

Getting yourself out of bed in the morning is one thing. Feeling prepared to face whatever comes your way that day is another. Where do you turn for a confidence-booster?

Believe it or not, one of the best confidence-builders you can find is your own two feet.

Researchers have discovered that regular exercise—thirty minutes, three or four times a week—boosts the confidence level of both men and women. This is due in part to the way exercise strengthens, tones, and improves the body's appearance. It also has to do with brain chemistry.

When a person exercises, changes take place inside the brain. Endorphins, released as one exercises, are proteins that work in the pleasure centers of the brain and make a person feel more exhilarated. When the heart rate increases during exercise, neurotrophins are also released, causing a person to feel more alert and focused.

Are you feeling anxious about your day? Take a walk, jog, cycle, or do some calisthenics first thing in the morning. See if you don't feel a little more on top of the world.

Those who exercise regularly also feel that if they can discipline themselves to exercise, they can discipline themselves to do just about anything!

The human body is one of the most awesome examples of God's creative power—an example we live with daily. He has created us not only to draw confidence from reading His Word and experiencing His presence through prayer, but also from the use of our body.

Put on those walking shoes and talk with God as you go! Not only will your body become more fit and your mind more alert, but the Holy Spirit will give you direction and peace about your day.

Let it be in God's own might
We gird us for the coming
fight, And, strong in him
whose cause is ours, In conflict
with unholy powers, We
grasp the weapons he has
given, The light and truth
and love of heaven.

JOHN GREENLEAF WHITTIER

PERSONAL IDEALS

What do you hold to be your personal ideals—the qualities you consider to be foremost in defining good character?

This is what Sir William Osler once said about his own ideals:

"I have three personal ideals. One, to do the day's work well and not to bother about tomorrow. . . . The second ideal has been to act the Golden Rule, as far as in me lay, toward my professional brethren and toward the patients committed to my care. And the third has been to cultivate such a measure of equanimity as would enable me to bear success with humility, the affection of my friends without pride, and to be ready when the day of sorrow and grief come to meet it with the courage befitting a man."

> He has shown you, O man, what is good; and what does the LORD require of you but to do justly, to love mercy, and to walk humbly with your God?
>
> MICAH 6:8 NKJV

A speech teacher once assigned her students to give a one-sentence speech, entitled "What I Would Like for My Tombstone to Read." The class told her later that this assignment was one of the most challenging assignments they had ever received. In virtually every case, the students saw a great discrepancy between the way they lived their lives and the way they desired their lives to be perceived by others.

Many of us make New Year's resolutions to "turn over a new leaf." We greet a new day with a vow or determination to "do better" in a certain area of our lives. But rarely do we give diligent thought to what we consider the highest and noblest pursuits in life.

Today, give some thought to what you hold to be the characteristics of a respected life. What do you aspire to in your own character?

As you identify these traits, you can then see more clearly how you desire to live your life and what must change in order to live up to your ideals.

Fame is vapor; popularity an accident, riches take wings. Only one thing endures and that is character.

HORACE GREELEY

MORE THAN POSITIVE THINKING

What we think about determines what we do. Even more important, the Scriptures tell us what we think about shapes our attitudes and how we live our lives.

The Greek city of Philippi was one of the places where the apostle Paul had a fruitful ministry. The Greeks were great thinkers. They loved a good debate, a lively conversation about philosophy, or a rousing time of oratory that might trigger the imagination. Paul wrote to the Philippians:

> Whatever things are true, whatever things are noble, whatever things are just, whatever things are pure, whatever things are lovely, whatever things are of good report, if there is any virtue and if there is anything praiseworthy—meditate on these things.

Philippians 4:8 NKJV

As he thinks in his heart, so is he.

PROVERBS 23:7 NKJV

It's interesting to note Paul wrote this immediately after addressing three other concerns in Philippians, chapter 4. First, he tells two women who are having an argument to become of "the same mind in the Lord." Paul wants them to be at peace with each other and to rejoice together in the Lord.

Second, Paul tells them to be gentle with all men. That's descriptive of having peace with those who don't know the Lord. And third, Paul advises them not to be anxious or worried about anything, but to turn all their troubles over to the Lord. He wants them to have total peace of mind and heart.

Paul is encouraging the Philippians to become God's "peace people" by turning their thoughts toward God's blessings and Word. He makes it very clear what the result will be: ". . . and the God of peace will be with you" (Philippians 4:9).

As we look for the good in others and meditate on the unending goodness of our Creator, we find the path toward peace with others and the peace that passes all understanding in whatever situation we find ourselves.

The mind grows by what it feeds on.

JOSIAH GILBERT HOLLAND

WINNING PREPARATION

The horse is made ready for the day
of battle, but victory rests with the LORD.

PROVERBS 21:31

Lexington, Kentucky, is renowned for producing the finest thoroughbred race horses in the world. More than 140 horse farms are located within the city limits and on the outskirts of the city. But it's not just the beautiful acreage that draws serious breeders to buy farms or horses in that area. The Kentucky Bluegrass area has something that cannot be found in such abundance anywhere else on earth—a particular type of limestone that lies just the right distance under the surface of the ground, continuously releasing vital minerals into the soil.

Plants grown in this soil, such as the grass the horses eat, are rich in the precise combination of minerals needed to build extremely strong but very light bones—ideal for racing. Thus, a colt eating Kentucky bluegrass spends his first two years eating exactly what will help him win the race of his life!

Along the same line, consider the habits of the Alaskan bull moose. The older males of the species battle for dominance during the fall breeding season, literally going head-to-head with their giant racks of antlers. Often the antlers, their only weapons, are broken. When this happens, the moose with the broken antlers will assuredly be defeated.

The heftiest moose with the largest and strongest antlers almost always triumphs. Therefore, the battle fought in the fall is really won in the summer when they do nothing but eat. The one that consumes the best diet for growing antlers and gaining weight will be the heavyweight in the fall. Those that eat inadequately have weaker antlers and less bulk.

There is a spiritual lesson here for all of us. Battles await us, and we must be prepared. Enduring faith, strength, and wisdom for trials can be developed before they are needed by spending time with God.

Choose today to steep yourself in God's Word and to spend time with Him in prayer. If troubles arise later, you will be attuned to your Father's voice and be able to get His battle plan—which is always the winning one!

I am sorry for men who do not read the Bible every day. I wonder why they deprive themselves of the strength and the pleasure.

WOODROW WILSON

JIGSAW PUZZLE

Are you a jigsaw puzzle afficionado?

If you have ever worked a complicated jigsaw puzzle, you know three things about them:

First, they take time. Few people can put several hundred pieces of a puzzle together rapidly. Most large and complex puzzles take several days, even weeks, to complete. The fun is in the process, the satisfaction in the accomplishment.

Second, the starting point of a puzzle is usually to identify the corners and edges, the pieces with a straight edge.

Third, jigsaw puzzles are fun to work by oneself but even more fun to work with others. When a "fit" is discovered between two or more pieces, the excitement is felt by all the participants.

Consider the day ahead of you to be like a piece in the jigsaw puzzle of your life. Indeed, its shape is likely to be just as jagged, its colors just as

Looking away [from all that will distract] to Jesus, Who is the Leader and the Source of our faith [giving the first incentive for our belief] and is also its Finisher [bringing it to maturity and perfection].

HEBREWS 12:2 AMP

unidentifiable. The meaning of today may not be sequential to that of yesterday. What you experience today may actually fit with something you experienced several months ago or something you will experience in the future. You aren't likely to see the big picture of your life by observing only one day. Even so, you can trust that there is a plan and purpose. All the pieces will come together according to God's design and timetable.

On some days, we find straight-edged pieces of our life's puzzle—truths that become a part of our reason for being. On other days, we find pieces that fit together, so we understand more about ourselves and about God's work in our lives. And on all days, we can know the joy of sharing our lives with others and inviting them to be part of the process of discovering who we are.

The main thing to remember is to enjoy the process. Live today to the fullest, knowing one day you'll see the full picture.

Faith is the daring of the soul
to go farther than it can see.

WILLIAM NEWTON CLARKE

WHICH LIFESTYLE?

The word "lifestyle" has been popular for several decades. In simplest terms, this word denotes how we live from a financial standpoint, the possessions we choose to buy, and how much money we have to spend.

A great deal is being written these days about the simple life—downshifting or downscaling. At the same time, we see an ongoing exaltation in our culture of all that is "excessive." As a nation, we seem to love peering into the lifestyles of the rich and famous. We envy them. Every few minutes television commercials tell us to buy more and better possessions.

The two paths—one toward a materially leaner life and the other toward a materially fatter life—are like opposite lanes on a highway. We are going either in one direction or the other. We are seeking to discard and downsize or to acquire and add.

"God so loved the World, that He gave."

JOHN 3:16 NASB

The Scriptures call us to neither a Spartan nor an opulent lifestyle, but rather to a lifestyle of generosity—a life without greed or hoarding. A life of giving freely, a life of putting everything we have at God's disposal. Our lifestyle is not about how much we earn, what we own, or where we travel and reside. It's how we relate to other people and how willing we are to share all we have with them.

In Visions of a World Hungry, Thomas G. Pettepiece offers this prayer: "Lord, help me choose a simpler lifestyle that promotes solidarity with the world's poor . . . affords greater opportunity to work together with my neighbors."

As you touch your various possessions throughout the day—from the things in your home to your clothing and your vehicle—ask yourself, "Would I be willing to loan, give, or share this with other people?" Then ask the even tougher question, "Do I actually share, loan, or give of my substance on a regular basis to others?"

Give what you have. To someone it may be better than you dare to think.

HENRY WADSWORTH LONGFELLOW

BEARING FRUIT

Meditate upon these things;
give thyself wholly to them;
that thy profiting may appear to all.

1 TIMOTHY 4:15 KJV

Two brothers were out walking on their father's vast acreage when they came upon a peach tree, its branches heavy with fruit. Each brother ate several juicy, tree-ripened peaches.

When they started toward the house, one brother gathered enough peaches for a delicious peach cobbler and several jars of jam. The second brother cut a limb from the tree to start a new peach tree. When this brother got home, he carefully tended the tree cutting until he could plant it outdoors. The branch took root and eventually produced healthy crops of peaches for him to enjoy year after year.

The Bible is like the fruit-bearing tree. Hearing the Word of God is like the first brother. He gathered fruit from hearing the Word and had enough to take home with him to eat later. But that doesn't compare with having your own peach tree in the backyard.

Memorizing the Word is like having the fruit tree in your backyard. It is there to nourish you all the time.

Scripture memorization is often considered a dull, burdensome task. But we could get highly motivated if we were given one hundred dollars for every Bible verse we memorized! The rewards of putting Scripture to memory may not always be monetary, but they are a far better treasure for life.

One of the greatest values of Scripture memorization is that it keeps us from sin. In Psalm 119:11 (NKJV) the psalmist wrote: "Your word I have hidden in my heart, that I might not sin against You."

For many people, the morning is the best time to memorize Scripture because one's mind is fresh, alert, and free from distractions. There are many different ways to memorize Scripture. Find the one that works best for you and begin hiding God's Word in your heart, so it may bring continual life and nourishment to you. This will produce fruit in your life which you can share with others.[22]

Sin will keep you from this book. This book will keep you from sin.

DWIGHT LYMAN MOODY

THE SKY'S THE LIMIT

People are often afraid that commitment to Jesus Christ means an endless list of "don'ts" and "thou shalt nots."

Highly motivated personalities are especially vulnerable to the lie that God's ways will restrict their creativity and growth. They fear they may never reach their full potential if they are tied to a lot of religious restrictions.

My yoke is easy, and my burden is light.

MATTHEW 11:30 KJV

Sadly, some of the smartest people on earth will never reach their full potential because they aren't tied to Jesus. The same holds for those who see His commands as "taking away all their fun." The fact is, true and lasting joy comes through knowing Jesus and following Him.

Consider this: You have watched a kite fly in the wind. Would you say the string that holds it is burdensome? No, it is there to control the kite. The kite will not fly unless it is in partnership with the string. The string and the kite are yoked together. You cannot cut the string and expect the kite to soar right up into the heavens. When the restrictive yoke of the string is cut, the kite may seem to fly freely for a moment, but it will soon crash to the ground.

The string gives the kite direction and purpose by sustaining its position against the wind and using the wind to its advantage. Without the string, the kite would be at the mercy of every passing influence and would doubtless end up being trapped in a tree or falling to the ground. When it is time for the kite to come to earth, the string gently reels it in, safely missing tree limbs and telephone poles.

In like manner, our daily surrender to the Lord Jesus is not burdensome, nor does it take away enjoyment in life. Like the kite string, He makes certain the wind is in our favor and we are always in position to get the most out of life.

Let Jesus be your "kite string" today, and see if you don't fly higher!

The greatness of a man's power is the measure of his surrender.

WILLIAM BOOTH

TAPROOTS

The art of raising miniature trees, known as bonsai, was developed by the Japanese. To create a miniature tree, the taproot is cut, forcing the tree to live on only the nourishment provided by the little roots growing along the surface of the soil. The tree lives, but it does not grow. Trees dwarfed in this way reach a height of only twelve to eighteen inches.

The taproot of a tree is the part of the root system that goes deep into the soil to absorb essential minerals and huge quantities of water—sometimes several hundred quarts a day. Taproots grow deepest in dry, sandy areas where there is little rainfall. The root system of a tree not only nourishes the tree but provides stability, anchoring it securely into the ground so it cannot be blown over by strong winds.

The root system is a good analogy for the Christian life. Richard J. Foster wrote, "Superficiality is the curse of our age. . . . The desperate need today is not for a greater number of intelligent people or gifted people but for deep people."

The Almighty . . . blesses you with blessings of the heavens above [and] blessings of the deep that lies below.

GENESIS 49:25

How do Christians grow deep in their spiritual life? In the same way a taproot grows deep—in search of the nourishment that will cause it to grow. In modern culture, Christians have to seek out spiritual food that will result in spiritual maturity. Regular times of prayer and Bible study, individual and corporate worship, serving others, and Christian fellowship are just some of the ways Christians can grow deep roots.

What are the benefits of depth in our spiritual life? Like the tree:

- We will be able to stand strong—"the righteous cannot be uprooted" (Proverbs 12:3).

- We will be fruitful—"the root of the righteous flourishes" (Proverbs 12:12).

Seek the Lord daily, so you can grow deep in your faith and withstand the storms of life.

A bit of the Book in the morning,
to order my onward way.
A bit of the Book in the evening,
to hallow the end of the day.

MARGARET SANGSTER

Watch Where
You're Goin'!

Do you not know that in a race all the
runners run, but only one gets the prize?
Run in such a way as to get the prize.

1 Corinthians 9:24

On March 6, 1987, Eamon Coughlan, the Irish
world record holder in the 1,500 meter, was competing
in a qualifying heat at the World Indoor Track
Championships in Indianapolis. With only two and a
half laps left, he was accidentally tripped by another
runner. Coughlan crashed onto the track, but with great
effort managed to get up, shake off the blow to his body,
and regain his stride. With an explosive burst of effort,
he managed to catch the leaders. Amazingly, with only
twenty yards left in the race, he was in third place, a
position good enough for him to qualify for the finals.

Just then, Coughlan looked over his shoulder to the
inside. When he didn't see anyone, he slowed his stride.
To his great surprise another runner, charging hard on
the outside, passed him only a yard before the finish line,
thus eliminating him from the final race. Coughlan's

great comeback effort was rendered worthless because he took his eyes off the finish line and assumed that his race would be run without further challenge.

Today you will face many distractions that have the potential to take your attention away from your goals. Some of those distractions will be of the small bump-in-the-road variety—minor, quickly-overcome annoyances along your path.

Others may be of the stumble-and-fall variety—those that seriously threaten your progress if you don't pick yourself up and move on. But the distraction that most seriously threatens your goal is the one that looks as if it is no threat at all: the I've-got-it-made-so-relax variety. It compels you to look over your shoulder, slow your pace, and take your eyes off the finish line.

The advice you were given early in life is still applicable today: Watch where you're goin'!

He that perseveres makes every difficulty an advancement and every contest a victory.

CHARLES CALEB COLTON

DOWNHILL FROM HERE

Jean-Claude Killy, the French ski champion, did more than work hard at his sport.

When he made his nation's ski team in the early 1960s, he was determined to be the best. He decided vigorous training was the key. Up at dawn each day, he ran up mountains with his skis on—a very painful activity. Weight training, sprinting—Killy was determined to do whatever it took to reach peak physical condition.

Other team members were working just as hard, and in the end it was a change in style, not conditioning, that set Killy apart.

The goal in ski racing is to ski down a prescribed mountain course faster than anyone else. Killy began experimenting to see if he could pare any seconds off his time. He found that if he skied with his legs apart, he had better balance. He also found that if he sat back on his skis when executing a turn, instead of leaning forward as was customary, he had better control,

Ye are a chosen generation, a royal priesthood, an holy nation, a peculiar people; that ye should shew forth the praises of him who hath called you out of darkness into his marvellous light.

1 PETER 2:9 KJV

which also resulted in faster times. Rather than regarding his ski poles as an accessory for balance, Killy tried using them to propel him forward.

Killy's style was unorthodox. But when he won most of the major ski events in 1966 and 1967, including three gold medals at the Winter Olympics, skiers around the world took notice. Today, the Killy style is the norm among downhill and slalom racers. Any other "style" would be considered odd.[23]

As Christians we are not called to conform to the world's standards, but to God's standards. Our lifestyle should challenge people to come to Jesus Christ and live according to His higher ways and purposes. The Christian "style" may seem odd to the unbeliever, but in the end, it is the style that will prevail!

Don't be afraid to be a little "unusual" today in the eyes of those who observe you. Your example may help win them over to a championship lifestyle.

The world is a net; the more we stir in it, the more we are entangled.

AUTHOR UNKNOWN

STAY THE COURSE

The Saturday of the dog sled derby dawned as a bright, clear, cold winter morning. The people of the small Wisconsin town on the southern shore of Lake Superior looked forward to the annual competition. The one-mile course across the ice had been marked out by little fir trees set into the surface of the frozen lake. Spectators standing on the steep slope along the shore had a good view of the entire course.

The contestants were all children—ranging from large, older boys with several dogs and big sleds to one little guy who appeared to be no more than five years old. He entered the race with a little sled pulled by his small dog and lined up with the rest of the entrants waiting for the race to begin.

When the signal was sounded declaring the start of the race, the racers took off in a flurry, and the youngest contestant with his little dog was quickly outdistanced. In fact, the larger and more experienced racers disappeared so quickly down the course that the little guy was hardly in the race at all. The contest was going well, however, and even though in last place, the little fellow stayed in the competition, enjoying every minute.

He [Jesus] stedfastly set his face to go to Jerusalem.

LUKE 9:51 KJV

About halfway around the course, the dog team that was in second began to overtake the team that was in the lead. The dogs came too close to the lead team, and soon the two teams were in a fight. Then, as each sled reached the fighting, snarling animals, they joined in the fracas.

None of the drivers seemed to be able to steer their teams clear of the growling brawl, and soon all of the dogs and racers became one big seething mass of kids, sleds, and dogs—all that is, but the little fellow and his one dog. He managed to stay the course and was the only one to finish the race.[24]

Each day holds the potential for something to side-track us from our intended purpose. No matter how great the distraction, we can finish the course if we stay focused and keep going!

If your determination is fixed,
I do not counsel you to despair.
Great works are performed not
by strength, but perseverance.

SAMUEL JOHNSON

RECIPROCITY

Pray for each other so
that you may be healed.

JAMES 5:16

Sometimes when we focus on helping others, we end up solving our own problems. That certainly was true for David, an eight-year-old from Wisconsin who had a speech impediment. His problem made him hesitant to read aloud or speak up in class.

David's mother also had a problem—multiple sclerosis. One winter day she and David were out walking, and her cane slipped on an icy patch, causing her to fall. She was unhurt, but the incident left David wishing he could do something to help her.

Some time later, David's teacher assigned her students to come up with an invention for a national contest. He decided he would invent a cane that wouldn't slide on ice by putting a nail on the bottom of it. After his mother expressed concern about the nail damaging floor coverings, he developed a retractable system. Much like a ball-point pen, the nail could be popped out of sight by releasing a button at the top of the cane.

David's invention earned him first prize in the contest. As the winner, he was required to make public appearances and communicate with those who expressed an interest in his project. The more he talked about the cane, the less noticeable his speech impediment became![25]

Who needs your help today?

They may not need you to invent something for them. They may simply need your assistance on a project, a word of encouragement, or prayer for a particular need. You will find, as you extend the effort, time, and energy to help someone, something inside you will be softened, healed, renewed, or strengthened. An outward expression toward others always does something inwardly that enables, empowers, and enhances the character of Christ Jesus in us.

That's God's principle of reciprocity!

If you pray for another, you will be helped yourself.

JEWISH PROVERB

THE VALUE OF ONE

Some days it's hard just to get out of bed. Our motivation is fading or completely gone. We are overcome with a "What difference does it make?" attitude. We become overwhelmed at the enormity of the duties before us. Our talents and resources seem minuscule in comparison to the task.

> "There is joy in the presence of the angels of God over one sinner who repents."
>
> LUKE 15:10 NASB

A businessman and his wife once took a much-needed getaway at an oceanside hotel. During their stay a powerful storm arose, lashing the beach and sending massive breakers against the shore. The storm woke the man. He lay still in bed listening to the storm's fury and reflecting on his own life of constant and continual demands and pressures.

Before daybreak the wind subsided. The man got out of bed to go outside and survey the damage done by the storm. He walked along the beach and noticed it was covered with starfish that had been thrown ashore by the massive waves. They lay helpless on the sandy beach. Unable to get to the water, the starfish faced inevitable death as the sun's rays dried them out.

Further down the beach, the man saw a figure walking along the shore. The figure would stoop and pick up something. In the dim of the early-morning twilight, he couldn't quite make it all out. As he approached he realized it was a young boy picking up the starfish one at a time and flinging them back into the ocean to safety.

As the man neared the young boy, he said, "Why are you doing that? One person will never make a difference—there are too many starfish to get back into the water before the sun comes up."

The boy said sadly, "Yes, that's true," and then bent to pick up another starfish. Then he said, "But I can sure make a difference to that one."

God never intended for an individual to solve all of life's problems. But He did intend for each one of us to use whatever resources and gifts He gave us to make a difference where we are.[26]

Small drops of water
hollow out a stone.

LUCRETIUS

PROCRASTINATION LEADS NOWHERE

Morning is a great time to make a list of things to do and plan the day. It's also the best time to tackle those tasks that are the most difficult or we like least. If we procrastinate as the day wears on, rationalization sets in, and sometimes even the tasks we had considered to be the most important are left undone.

Here's a little poem just for those who struggle with procrastination:

How and When

We are often greatly bothered
By two fussy little men,
>Who sometimes block our pathway
>Their names are How and When.

If we have a task or duty
Which we can put off awhile,
And we do not go and do it
>You should see those two rogues smile!

But there is a way to beat them,
And I will tell you how:

I will hasten and not delay to obey your commands.

PSALM 119:60

186

If you have a task or duty,
Do it well, and do it now.

—Unknown

As part of your morning prayer time, ask the Lord to help you to overcome any tendency to procrastinate and prioritize projects according to His plans and purposes.

Often we ask the Lord, "What do You want me to do?" but then fail to ask Him one of the key follow-up questions, "When do You want me to do this?" When we have a sense of God's timing, and in some cases His urgency about a matter, our conviction grows to get the job done right away.

God's "omnipresence" means He is always with you, and He is always "timely." He's with you in the "now" moments of your life. He is concerned with how you use every moment of your time. Recognize that He desires to be part of your time-management and task-completion process today!

Nothing is so fatiguing as the eternal hanging on of an uncompleted task.

WILLIAM JAMES

A CORK'S INFLUENCE

Let us behave decently, as in the
daytime . . . clothe yourselves
with the Lord Jesus Christ.

ROMANS 13:13-14

A tour group passed through a particular room in a factory. They viewed an elongated bar of steel, which weighed five hundred pounds, suspended vertically by a chain. Near it, an average-size cork was suspended by a silk thread.

"You will see something shortly that is seemingly impossible," said an attendant to the group of sightseers. "This cork is going to set this steel bar in motion!"

She took the cork in her hand, pulled it only slightly to the side of its original position, and released it. The cork swung gently against the steel bar, which remained motionless.

For ten minutes the cork, with pendulum-like regularity, struck the iron bar. Finally, the bar vibrated slightly. By the time the tour group passed through the room an hour later, the great bar was swinging like the pendulum of a clock!

Many of us feel we are not exerting a feather's weight of influence upon others or making a dent in the bastions of evil in the world. Not so! Sometimes we don't realize how powerful the cumulative influence of God's goodness which we walk in is to those around us.

Not everyone is called to spread the love of Jesus through the pulpit, on the evangelistic trail, or in a full-time counseling ministry. Most of us are called to live our lives as "corks," through word and example—quietly, gently tapping away through the work of our daily lives. Tap by loving tap, in God's time, even the quietest Christian can make a huge difference in the lives of those whom preachers may never reach.

One modern-day philosopher has estimated that the average person encounters at least twenty different people in the course of a day, with a minimum of eye contact and exchange of words or gesture. That's at least twenty opportunities for a cork to "tap" at the collective human heart.

As you go about your day, remember that even a smile can warm a stranger's heart and draw him to Jesus.

The entire ocean is affected
by a pebble.

BLAISE PASCAL

EARLY TO BED

Most of us are familiar with the old saying: "Early to bed and early to rise, makes a man healthy and wealthy and wise." And there are numerous references in the Bible to the joys and benefits of rising early. The psalmist said,

> "My heart is steadfast, O God, my heart is steadfast;
>> I will sing and give praise.
>> Awake, my glory!
>>> Awake, lute and harp! I will awaken the dawn."
>
> Psalm 57:7-8 NKJV

> O God, You are my God; early will I seek You.
>
> PSALM 63:1 NKJV

The clear implication is that the psalmist had a habit of getting up before dawn and "singing in" the morning. But what does this have to do with our sunset hours?

Very practically speaking, in order to be able to rise early in the morning, we have to get to bed early. There is no substitute for sleep. According to modern sleep research, most people need seven to ten hours of sleep a day, and lost hours can never be made up.

Sufficient sleep is the foremost factor in a person's ability to sustain a high performance level, cope with stress, and feel a sense of satisfaction in life. Getting enough sleep directly impacts our moods and emotions, our ability to think creatively and respond quickly, and our ability to sustain exertion. It is as vital to our health as what we eat and drink.

More good news about sleep and our health is that every hour of sleep we get before midnight is twice as beneficial as the hours after midnight!

A good night's sleep is one of God's blessings to you. Sufficient sleep was a part of His design for your body and His plan for your life. When you make a habit of retiring early, you put yourself in a position to receive this blessing. You'll find it easier to rise early and seek the Lord for wisdom and strength for the day ahead.

Tired nature's sweet restorer, balmy sleep

EDWARD YOUNG

THE NIGHT SKY

When was the last time you gazed up into the star-filled sky on a clear night? Do you wonder what it would be like to travel in the heavens among the stars? What lies beyond what your physical eyes can see?

Jamie Buckingham described a night like that in the snowy mountains of North Carolina:

"I walked up the dark, snow-covered road toward Cowee Bald. The sky had cleared, revealing a billion stars twinkling in the clear, cold night. The only sound was the gurgling of a small mountain stream beside the road and the soft crunch of my shoes in the snow. All the other night noises were smothered, leaving me with the impression of standing alone on earth.

I consider thy heavens, the work of thy fingers, the moon and the stars, which thou hast ordained.

PSALM 8:3 KJV

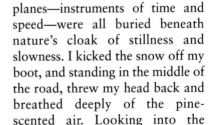

"I wondered about the time, but to glance at my watch would have been sacrilegious. Clocks, calendars, automobiles, and airplanes—instruments of time and speed—were all buried beneath nature's cloak of stillness and slowness. I kicked the snow off my boot, and standing in the middle of the road, threw my head back and breathed deeply of the pine-scented air. Looking into the heavens I could see stars whose light had left there a million years ago, and realized I was just glimpsing the edge of space. Beyond that was infinity—and surrounding it all, the Creator.

"I remembered a quote from the German philosopher Kant. Something about two irrefutable evidences of the existence of God: the moral law within and the starry universe above. I breathed His name: 'God.'

"Then, overwhelmed by His presence, I called Him what I had learned to call Him through experience: 'Father!'"[27]

Tonight, contemplate the stars in the heavens. You will find there a glimpse of eternity. What an awesome thought: The Creator of the universe invites me to have a personal relationship with Him!

> The more I study nature, the more I am amazed at the Creator.
>
> LOUIS PASTEUR

TRUE RICHES

Don't store up treasures on earth!

MATTHEW 6:19 CEV

They were married as soon as they graduated from college. They both were smart, attractive, and voted "most likely to succeed" by their peers. Within two decades, they had reached some pretty lofty rungs on the ladder of success: three children who attended private schools, a mansion, two luxury cars, a vacation house on the lake, a prolific investment portfolio, and the respect of all who knew them. If you had asked them what was most important in life, they would have reeled off a list of all they owned, the places they had been, and the things they had done. Success was sweet, and money made their world go round.

It will probably come as no surprise to you to learn that one day the bottom dropped out of this couple's life. They had personally guaranteed a business loan, assuming that their partners were as trustworthy as they. Not so. One partner embezzled nearly half a million dollars, and this Couple Who Had It All started down the road to becoming the Couple Who Lost It All. In the midst of their problems, the police came to their door late one night to tell them their oldest son had been killed in a car accident.

This couple discovered something vitally important in the course of putting their lives back together. A neighbor invited them to church, and thinking that they had nothing to lose by going, they started attending, eventually becoming regular members. To their amazement, they found they were enjoying Bible study, making lots of genuine friends, and feeling accepted for who they were—not for what they had in the way of material possessions. Their children also found a place to belong (no designer jeans required).[28]

Ideally, none of us will have to lose it all in order to find it all. In fact, our Heavenly Father wants us to live abundantly. Keeping our priorities straight, remembering to put God first and others ahead of ourselves, is the key to sweet sleep at night!

Building one's life on a foundation of gold is just like building a house on foundations of sand.

HENRIK IBSEN

Everyday Needs

"Oh, no! We're going to have to run for the ferry again!" Elaine cried. "And, unless we find a parking place in the next minute or two, we're never going to make it!"

As Elaine and her daughter, Cathy, struggled through the downtown Seattle traffic, she thought back to when they had moved to Bainbridge Island four years earlier. They had thought it to be a perfect, idyllic place, and it was while her daughter was in high school and she could work part time at home.

Now college bills had made full-time work a necessity for Elaine. She, her husband, and Cathy were obliged to make the daily commute to Seattle via the ferry. With a car parked on both sides of the water, praying for parking spaces had become a daily event.

"I told you we needed to get away from your office sooner," Cathy chided. "You just can't count on finding a parking place

> This is the confidence we have in approaching God: that if we ask anything according to his will, he hears us. And if we know that he hears us—whatever we ask—we know that we have what we asked of him.
>
> 1 John 5:14-15

within walking distance of the ferry when the water-front is full of summer tourists and conventioneers!"

"God knew about that last-minute customer I had, and He knows we have to make this ferry in order to get home in time to fix dinner and make it to the church meeting," Elaine assured her. Then she prayed aloud, "Lord, we'll circle this block one more time. Please have someone back out, or we're not going to make it."

"Mom, there it is!" Cathy shouted, as they rounded the last corner. "Those people just got in their car. I have to admit—sometimes you have a lot more faith than I do. Who'd think God would be interested in whether or not we find a parking place?"

"But that's the exciting part of it," Elaine explained. "God is interested in every part of our lives—even schedules and parking places. Now, let's run for it!"[29]

The Lord knows all the circumstances of your day—and your tomorrow. Trust Him to be the "Lord of the details."

Anything large enough for a wish to light upon is large enough to hang a prayer on.

GEORGE MACDONALD

CRADLED

A number of years ago, two young women boarded a ferry to cross the English Channel from England to France. About halfway through their five-hour journey, the ferry hit rough waters, and a crew member later told them they were experiencing one of the roughest seas of the year! The ferry tossed about rather violently on the waves, to the point where even the seasoned crew felt ill.

At the time the ferry hit rough water, the two women were eating a light lunch in the back of the boat. They quickly put their sandwiches away. One woman lamented, "It's hard to eat while you're riding on the back of a bucking bronco!"

Now will I arise, saith the LORD; I will set him in safety from him that puffeth at him.

PSALM 12:5 KJV

When it became apparent that the pitching of the boat was not going to abate, one of the women decided to return to her assigned seat in the middle of the ferry. She soon fell sound asleep and experienced no more sea sickness. Toward the end of the trip, after the ferry had moved into calmer waters off the coast of France, the other woman joined her. "That was awful," she exclaimed. "I was nauseous for two hours!"

"I'm sorry to hear that," said the second woman, almost ashamed to admit that she hadn't suffered as her friend had.

"Weren't you sick?" the first woman asked in amazement. "No," her friend admitted. "Here at our seats I must have been at the fulcrum of the boat's motion. I could see the front and back of the boat were moving up and down violently, but here, the motion was relatively calm. I simply imagined myself being rocked in the arms of God, and I fell asleep."

All around you today, life may have been unsettling and stormy, your entire life bouncing about on rough waters. But when you return to the "center" of your life, the Lord, He will set you in safety. Let Him rock you gently to sleep, and trust Him to bring you through the rough waters tomorrow.

No sleep can be tranquil unless
the mind is at rest.

LUCIUS ANNAEUS SENECA

TIGHTROPE TRUST

I know whom I have believed,
and am persuaded that he is able to
keep that which I have committed
unto him against that day.

2 TIMOTHY 1:12 KJV

In the mid-nineteenth century, tightrope walker Blondin was going to perform his most daring feat yet. He stretched a two-inch steel cable across Niagara Falls. As he did, a large crowd gathered to watch. He asked the onlookers, "How many of you believe that I can carry the weight of a man on my shoulders across this gorge?"

The growing crowd shouted and cheered, believing that he could perform this difficult feat. Blondin picked up a sack of sand that weighed about 180 pounds and carried it across the Falls. They both arrived on the other side safely.

Then Blondin asked, "How many of you believe that I can actually carry a person across the gorge?" Again, the crowd cheered him on.

"Which one of you will climb on my shoulders and let me carry you across the Falls?" Silence fell across the crowd. Everyone wanted to see Blondin carry a person across the gorge, but nobody wanted to put his life into Blondin's hands.

Finally, a volunteer came forward willing to participate in this death-defying stunt. Who was this person? It was Blondin's manager, who had known the tightrope walker personally for many years.

As they prepared to cross the Falls, Blondin instructed his manager, "You must not trust your own feelings, but mine. You will feel like turning when we don't need to turn. And if you trust your feelings, we will both fall. You must become part of me." The two made it across to the other side safely.[30]

Jesus gives us the same instruction when we are asked to trust Him in difficult circumstances: "Don't trust your own feelings, trust Me to carry you through."

All I have seen teaches me to trust the Creator for all I have not seen.

RALPH WALDO EMERSON

UNIQUELY FASHIONED

As you lie in bed tonight, stretch your limbs in all directions and then relax for a moment to ponder the fact that your body has been fearfully and wonderfully made. The word "fearfully" in this context is like the word of supreme quality that has been popular among teens in recent years, "Awesome!"

When you stop to think about all the intricate details involved in the normal functioning of your body—just one creation among countless species and organisms on the planet—you must conclude, "The Designer of this piece of work had a marvelous plan."

> I will praise thee;
> for I am fearfully
> and wonderfully
> made; marvellous
> are thy works;
> and that my
> soul knoweth
> right well.
>
> PSALM 139:14 KJV

Listen to your heartbeat. Flex your fingers and toes. Keep in mind as you do that:

- no one else among all humanity has your exact fingerprints, handprints, or footprints,

- no one else has your voiceprint,

- no one else has your genetic code—the exact positioning of the many genes that define your physical characteristics.

Furthermore, nobody else has your exact history in time and space. Nobody else has gone where you've gone, done what you've done, said what you've said, or created what you have created. You are truly a one-of-a-kind masterpiece.

The Lord knows precisely how you were made and why you were made. When something in your life goes amiss, He knows how to fix it. When you err or stray from His commandments, He knows how to woo you back and work even the worst tragedies and mistakes for your good when you repent.

You have been uniquely fashioned for a specific purpose on the earth. He has a "design" for your life. It is His own imprint, His own mark. Make a resolution in these night hours to be true to what the Lord has made you to be and to become.

Man is heaven's masterpiece.

FRANCIS QUARLES

MY KINGDOM FOR SOME SLEEP

In the recent past, the Internal Revenue Service received an envelope with one hundred $100 bills in it—no name, no address, no note—just money. Someone was feeling guilty.

On another day, the IRS received a large box containing a stack of handmade quilts. The note said, "Please sell these and use the money to settle my tax bill." Since the IRS isn't in the business of selling craft items, the quilts had to be returned.

> Let us draw near to God with a sincere heart in full assurance of faith, having our hearts sprinkled to cleanse us from a guilty conscience.
>
> HEBREWS 10:22

One man believed he owed the U.S. District Court $15.43. The court case in question had been held eighteen years earlier, and the man just couldn't wrestle with his conscience any longer. The court insisted that the man didn't owe the money, but he refused to take no for an answer.

Another woman wrote to the IRS and said she felt guilty about cheating on her taxes; enclosed was a check. "If I still can't sleep," she said, "I'll send more."

The Bible has much to say about the blessings of a clear conscience and the agony of a guilty one. Perhaps the best example of a man who paid heed to his conscience was David. He made many mistakes, but he always admitted it when he did wrong. He was a man who couldn't sleep until he made peace with his Maker.

"For I know my transgressions, and my sin is always before me," he said. "Against you, you only, have I sinned and done what is evil in your sight, so that you are proved right when you speak and justified when you judge" (Psalm 51:3-4).

Are we as honest about our shortcomings as David was?

Confessing our sins brings release from guilt, peace of mind, and sweet sleep. As you retire for the night, check your heart. If you find any unconfessed sin, ask the Lord for forgiveness, and He will give it. He is faithful and just to forgive you from your sins, and He will cleanse you from all unrighteousness (1 John 1:9 KJV).

> A fault confessed is a new
> virtue added to a man.
>
> JAMES S. KNOWLES

DEAL WITH IT!

Be ye angry, and sin not: let not the
sun go down upon your wrath.

EPHESIANS 4:26 KJV

One of the most controversial events in America occurred when Bernard Goetz had had enough and decided he wasn't going to take it anymore. He did what many people have wanted to do—he fought back and pulled a gun when he was attacked on the subway.

Goetz' action received an outpouring of support. He touched a nerve in people who had simply had enough of other people threatening their lives. Criticism comes, however, when we allow guns in the hands of angry, violent people. As Christians, anger can be a terrible enemy.

The beginnings of anger almost go unnoticed: petty irritations, ordinary frustrations, minor aggravations—things we experience daily. Then these small things start adding up. Pressures build and turn into rage. Without relief, pent-up anger can turn violent, with devastating consequences.

How do we keep our passions from becoming uncontrolled anger? How should we defuse the anger that makes us want to retaliate?

There is a righteous, Godly anger that energizes us to action, to right the wrong, to defend the innocent.

However, anger becomes sin when it turns to hate and retribution. Then it is often expressed in inappropriate, destructive ways. We can fly off the handle and act in ways that are as hurtful as what caused us to be angry in the first place. Worse yet, we can store up anger and become bitter and resentful.

An old proverb says, "He who goes angry to bed has the devil for a bedfellow." This is not a condition for sweet sleep!

There are several things we can do to take control of our anger before it takes control of us:

1. Yell at God first! He already knows you're upset.
2. Ask God to give you understanding about the situation, to show you the root of your anger, if that's the case.
3. Turn the situation over to God. Forgive those who have hurt you, and let Him deal with them. Turn His power loose in the circumstances.
4. Don't do anything without having complete inner peace from His Spirit.

Then you can sleep easily at night, knowing God can turn anything around to work for your good.

I was angry with my friend. I told my wrath, my wrath did end. I was angry with my foe. I told it not, my wrath did grow.

WILLIAM BLAKE

UNIQUELY POSITIONED

A number of years ago, IMAX filmmakers produced a movie titled Cosmos. In it, they explored the "edges" of creation—both outer space as viewed through the most powerful telescope and inner space as viewed through the most powerful microscope. Viewers saw for themselves that at the far reaches of space, clumps of matter (huge stars) seem to be suspended in fixed motion and separated by vast areas of seemingly empty blackness.

> When I consider your heavens, the work of your fingers, the moon and the stars, which you have set in place, what is man that you are mindful of him?
>
> PSALM 8:3-4

They also saw that the same can be said for the depths of inner space—clumps of matter are suspended in fixed orbits, separated by vast areas of seemingly empty blackness. In fact, the world of the distant stars is almost identical in appearance and form to the world of the tiniest neutrinos! Furthermore, neither of these "edges" of creation has been explored fully. Both inner and outer space appear as if they may very well extend into infinity.

In sharp contrast, the created earth as we experience it daily is uniquely suspended between these two opposite poles. Our world is filled with varied colors, dynamic forms, differing patterns, changing seasons, and adaptable functions.

It is as if God has placed man at the very center of His vast creation, with the maximum amount of complexity, meaning, and choice. We are "hung in the balances" literally, as well as figuratively—the pivot point between the great and the small, the vastness of outer space and the vastness of inner space.

We are not only fearfully and wonderfully made, but we are fearfully and wonderfully positioned in God's creation. The Lord has a place for mankind and specifically, He has a place for you. Thank God for your uniqueness today. Delight in all that makes you special in His eyes. Praise Him for all that He has designed you to be, to become, and to give.

> When God conceived the world, that was poetry. He formed it, and that was sculpture. He colored it, and that was painting. He peopled it with living beings, and that was the grand, divine, eternal drama.
>
> DAVID BELASCO

Not Exactly Puppy Love

Aaron and Abbey had been happily married for nearly a year when Aaron bought Abbey a "present" she never wanted: a great big Chow puppy with paws the size of baseballs.

"Aaron, darling," Abbey said with conviction, "dogs and I are natural enemies. We just don't get along!"

"But Abs!" Aaron used his pet name for her hoping to soften her up, "You'll get used to him." It was pretty clear to them that the puppy was really a present for Aaron.

"Pup," as he came to be called, won an uneasy spot in their household. Determined that the dog should understand his place as her enemy, Abbey silently launched a campaign against him.

I say unto you,

Love your

enemies.

Matthew 5:44 KJV

Pup sensed her resistance and reciprocated for a while by stealing towels, tearing up shoes and furniture, and carrying off whatever small object Abbey was using the minute she turned away. He completely ignored her attempts to correct him. So went Pup's first year in the family.

Then one day Abbey noticed a change in Pup's approach. To her astonishment, he began greeting her joyously each time she came home, nudging her hand and licking her fingers in a friendly "hello." Whenever she had to feed him, he sat for a moment and gazed at her adoringly before he began eating. To top it off, he began accompanying her on her early morning walks, staying close at her side to ward off other dogs as she walked down their deserted road.

Little by little, Pup loved Abbey into a humbling truce. Today, Abbey says that Pup's persistence has taught her a lot about loving her enemies. She says Pup is winning—but don't tell Aaron.[31]

Is there someone you know—perhaps even someone in your own family—who needs an expression of your love, rather than your resistance?

We should conduct ourselves toward our enemy as if he were one day to be our friend.

CARDINAL JOHN HENRY NEWMAN

WHAT WOULD YOU SAY?

"You are the salt of the earth. . . .
You are the light of the world."

MATTHEW 5:13-14 RSV

Standing in line with his squad in the Red Army, Taavi had already made up his mind what he was going to say. The officers made their way toward him, interrogating each soldier down the line with the same question: "Are you a Christian?" "No," came the answer back. Then to the next one: "Are you a Christian?" "No," was the response.

The young conscripts stood at attention, their eyes fixed ahead. The questioners got closer to the eighteen-year-old Estonian who had been drafted into the Red Army during the Soviet occupation of his country.

Taavi had long been a Christian. Although only the older people were permitted to go to church in his country, Taavi's grandmother had shared her faith with her young grandson. He had accepted the Lord as his Savior, and although he wasn't allowed to attend church, his grandmother taught him what she had learned each week.

The questioners neared. Taavi never really had any doubt what answer he would give. His mind had been made up years before, but he was still nervous. When the officers reached his place in line, they asked, "Are you a Christian?" Without flinching, Taavi said in a clear voice, "Yes."

"Then come with us," ordered the commanding officers.

Taavi followed them immediately. They got in a vehicle and drove to the building that housed the kitchen and mess hall. Taavi had no idea what was about to transpire, but he obeyed their orders.

The officers said to him, "We are taking you out of combat preparation. You are a Christian and you will not steal, so we will put you in the kitchen." The kitchen was the biggest black-market operation in the Red Army, with the smuggling and illegal sale of food to hungry soldiers. They knew Taavi's presence would reduce the amount of theft.

When you are challenged for your faith, rise up and boldly proclaim the truth. God will be with you, and He will reward you for your faithfulness.

If we are correct and right in our Christian life at every point, but refuse to stand for the truth at a particular point where the battle rages—then we are traitors to Christ.

MARTIN LUTHER

AFTER DARKNESS, DAWN

At the turn of the century, there was a city worker whose youth had been spent in evil ways. But one night during a revival meeting he was spiritually born anew. Soon after, he ran into one of his old drinking pals. Knowing his friend needed Jesus, he attempted to witness to him about his newly found peace. His friend rebuffed him rudely and made fun of him for "turning pious."

> You are a chosen people, a royal priesthood, a holy nation, a people belonging to God, that you may declare the praises of him who called you out of darkness into his wonderful light.
>
> 1 PETER 2:9

"I'll tell you what," said the new Christian, "you know that I am the city lamplighter. When I go 'round turning out the lights, I look back, and all the road over which I've been walking is blackness. That's what my past is like."

He went on, "I look on in front, and there's a long row of twinkling lights to guide me, and that's what the future is like since I found Jesus."

"Yes," says the friend, "but by-and-by you get to the last lamp and turn it out, and where are you then?"

"Then," said the Christian, "why, when the last lamp goes out, it's dawn, and there ain't no need for lamps when the morning comes."

Many children carry their fear of the dark into adulthood in the form of other kinds of fears—fear of failure, rejection, loss, pain, loneliness, or disappointment. Each of these fears seems to grow in darkness. Darkness is a metaphor for many things: death, night, uncertainty, evil—but in all of them, Jesus is the Light that brings illumination and comfort.

When light shines, not only is darkness eliminated, but fears are relieved. Indeed, not only does Jesus give you as much light as you need to proceed in faith, but because of His sacrifice at Calvary, you can be assured of His eternal dawn when the last lamp goes out! Like the lamplighter said, "And there ain't no need for lamps when the morning comes."

Christ has turned all our sunsets into dawns.

CLEMENT OF ALEXANDRIA

LETTING GO

The spider monkey is a tiny animal native to South and Central America. Quick as lightning, it is a very difficult animal to capture in the wild. For years, people attempted to shoot spider monkeys with tranquilizer guns or capture them with nets, but they discovered the monkeys were nearly always faster than their fastest draw or quickest trap.

Then somebody discovered the best method for capturing this elusive creature. They found that if you take a clear, narrow-mouthed glass bottle, put one peanut inside it, and wait, you can catch a spider monkey.

What happens? The spider monkey reaches into the bottle to get the peanut, and he can't get his hand out of the bottle as long as it is clenching the peanut. The bottle is so heavy in proportion to his size, he can't drag it with him—and the spider monkey is too persistent to let go of a peanut once he has grasped it. In fact, you can dump a wheel barrow full of peanuts or bananas right next to him, and he won't let go of that one peanut.

Forgetting those things which are behind, and reaching forth unto those things which are before, I press toward the mark for the prize of the high calling of God in Christ Jesus.

PHILIPPIANS 3:13-14 KJV

How many of us are like that? Unwilling to change a habit, be a little flexible, try a new method, or give up something we know is bringing destruction to our lives, we stubbornly cling to our way, even if it brings pain and suffering.

Today, don't cling to a negative situation that may be draining you of your full vitality, energy, creativity, and enthusiasm for living. As the well-known phrase advises, "Let go, and let God!"

Trust the Lord to lead you to the wise counsel and new opportunities He has for you. Have faith in Him to provide what you truly need to live a peaceful, balanced, and fulfilling life. You may never lose your taste for peanuts, but with the Lord's help you can discern when they are trapped in glass bottles!

Finish every day and be done with it. You have done what you could. Some blunders and absurdities no doubt have crept in; forget them as soon as you can. Tomorrow is a new day; begin it well and serenely and with too high a spirit to be cumbered with your old nonsense. This day is all that is good and fair. It is too dear, with its hopes and invitations, to waste a moment on yesterdays.

RALPH WALDO EMERSON

Running on Empty

There remains, then, a Sabbath-rest for the people of God; for anyone who enters God's rest also rests from his own work, just as God did from his.

Hebrews 4:9-10

Some years ago, a research physician made an extensive study of the amount of oxygen a person needs throughout the day. He was able to demonstrate that the average workman breathes thirty ounces of oxygen during a day's work, but he uses thirty-one. At the close of the day he is one ounce short, and his body is tired.

He goes to sleep and breathes more oxygen than he uses to sleep, so in the morning he has regained five-sixths of the ounce he was short. The night's rest does not fully balance the day's work!

By the seventh day, he is six-sixths or one whole ounce in debt again. He must rest an entire day to replenish his body's oxygen requirements.

Further, he demonstrated that replenishing an entire ounce of oxygen requires thirty to thirty-six hours (one twenty-four-hour day plus the preceding and following nights) when part of the resting is done while one is awake and moving about.

Over time, failure to replenish the oxygen supply results in the actual death of cells and, eventually, the premature death of the person.

A person is restored as long as he or she takes the seventh day as a day of rest.[32]

Sound familiar? The God who created us not only invites us to rest, He created our bodies in such a fashion that they demand rest.

Most people think that "keeping the Sabbath" is solely an act of devotion to God. But in turning your attention to Him, He can offer you true rest and replenishment in every area of your life—spirit, soul, and body. He is not only our daily strength, He is our source of rest, recreation, and replenishment.

Take rest; a field that has rested gives a bountiful crop.

OVID

SHINING THROUGH

A little girl was among a group of people being given a guided tour through a great cathedral. As the guide explained the various parts of the structure—the altar, the choir, the screen, and the nave—the little girl's attention was intently focused on a stained glass window.

For a long time she silently pondered the window. Looking up at the various figures, her face was bathed in a rainbow of color as the afternoon sun poured into the transept of the huge cathedral.

"Let your light so shine before men, that they may see your good works and glorify your Father in heaven."

MATTHEW 5:16 NKJV

As the group was about to move on, she gathered enough courage to ask the tour conductor a question. "Who are those people in that pretty window?"

"Those are the saints," the guide replied.

That night, as the little girl was preparing for bed, she told her mother proudly: "I know who the saints are."

"Oh?" replied the mother. "And just who are the saints?"

Without a moment's hesitation the little girl replied: "They are the people who let the light shine through!"[33]

As you look back over your day, did you let God's light shine through? Sometimes we pass by these opportunities saying, "It will just take too much out of me." But the Bible lets us know that everything we give will come back to us—multiplied (Luke 6:38 KJV).

We see this principle in nature. A microscopic speck of radium can send out a stream of sparks which give off light and heat, yet in emitting the light and heat, it does not deplete itself of its own energy.

As Christians we are called to share the light of Jesus in a world of darkness. Like rays of light that break through gloom and darkness, we can bring hope and encouragement.

Remember, the light of your life gives those around you a glimpse of Jesus, the Source of eternal and constant light. As you let your light shine, it will grow brighter!

Should first my lamp spread
light and purest rays bestow
The oil must then from you,
my dearest Jesus, flow.

ANGELUS SILESIUS

THE POWER OF
FORGIVENESS

Unforgiveness is a destructive and insidious force, having more effect on the one who is unforgiving than on the unforgiven. A great example of this was an experience of one of the outstanding intellects of all history, Leonardo da Vinci.

Just before he commenced work on his depiction of the Last Supper, he had a violent quarrel with a fellow painter. Leonardo was so enraged and bitter, he determined to use the face of his enemy as the face of Judas, thus taking his revenge by handing down the man to succeeding generations in infamy and scorn.

"If you forgive men when they sin against you, your heavenly Father will also forgive you."

MATTHEW 6:14

The face of Judas was, therefore, one of the first that he finished, and everyone readily recognized it as the face of the painter with whom he had quarreled.

However, when he attempted to paint the face of Jesus Christ, Leonardo could make no progress. Something seemed to be baffling him—holding him back and frustrating his efforts. At length, he came to the conclusion that what was hindering and frustrating him was that he had painted his enemy into the face of Judas.

When he painted over the face of his enemy in the portrait of Judas, he commenced anew on the face of Jesus. This depiction became a success which has been acclaimed through the ages.

You cannot be painting the features of Jesus Christ into your own life and at the same time be painting another face with the colors of enmity and hatred.

If you are harboring unforgiveness and bitterness, forgive your offender and put him or her and the situation in God's hands. Ask Him to cleanse you of those negative feelings and to release you from their bondage. As you forgive, you will be forgiven and set free to live your life with inner peace.

He that demands mercy, and shows none, ruins the bridge over which he himself is to pass.

THOMAS ADAMS

OUT OF SIGHT

Just as you received Christ Jesus as
Lord, continue to live in him, rooted
and built up in him, strengthened
in the faith as you were taught,
and overflowing with thankfulness.

COLOSSIANS 2:6-7

A tree is nothing without its roots, and for the most part they do their job underground. Young roots absorb water and minerals from the soil. Older roots take these materials and send them into the stem.

In order to keep the tree going during dormant periods, the roots store food, similar to the way a bear builds bulk to get him through hibernation. Food stored in the tree's roots provides energy and food needed when the weather changes and it's time for new growth.

Trees never stop growing. As long as they live, some type of growth is taking place. New roots are forming, new branches are appearing, or old bark is being sloughed off so that new bark can take its place. Without the roots to lend mechanical support, act as anchors, and store food, a tree would fall.

The God who cares enough about trees to set up an intricate feeding system for them gives each of us the food, water, and air we require to survive. He gives us family and friends, opportunities, and provision to accomplish His plan for our lives. We can't see God with our physical eyes, but like the finely developed web of roots beneath the ground, we know He's there, working on our behalf. That is His nature as Jehovah Jireh—the God who provides.

Have you ever been hungry? Jesus is the bread of life; He promises that whoever comes to Him will never go hungry (John 6:35 KJV).

Have you ever been thirsty? As Jesus told the Samaritan woman at the well, "Whoever drinks the water I give him will never thirst" (John 4:14).

Do you ever find yourself gasping for breath? Job knew who to thank for the air we all breathe. "In his hand is the life of every creature and the breath of all mankind" (Job 12:10).

Stay rooted in the Lord and watch Him provide for your every need!

He that so much for you
did do, Will do yet more.

THOMAS WASHBOURNE

NO LONGER ENEMIES

The orange kitten was hungry. The grizzly bear was lonely. The man was apprehensive.

The cat weighed no more than ten ounces when he first slid under the fence into the bear's pen. The man was almost in a panic thinking the hungry grizzly would kill him with one swat and eat him for dinner—carnivorous bears make much larger animals a part of their diet.

The grizzly, whose name was Griz, had come to the Oregon wildlife center in 1990 when he was just a cub. Hit by a train while foraging on railroad tracks in Montana, he suffered severe head injuries and was deemed unfit to return to the wild.

The kitten was one of four kittens abandoned at the center early in the summer. Volunteers were able to find homes for the rest of the litter, but Cat, as he was now called, somehow eluded them.

Then one day in July, Cat turned up in Griz's pen. Afraid to do anything that might alarm Griz, the man just watched, expecting the worst. As the 650-pound grizzly was eating his midday meal,

The wolf also shall dwell with the lamb, and the leopard shall lie down with the kid; and the calf and the young lion and the fatling together; and a little child shall lead them.

Isaiah 11:6 KJV

something extraordinary happened. The bear very gently picked out a chicken wing with his forepaw and dropped it near Cat.

From that moment on, Griz and Cat became something of a slapstick animal act. Cat would lay in ambush, then leap out and swat Griz on his nose. Griz would carry Cat in his mouth. Cat would ride on Griz's back, and sometimes Griz would lick Cat.

Their friendly relationship defies both the patterns of nature as well as their own troubled life histories. Griz never took advantage of Cat's weaknesses, and each animal has accommodated the other's needs.[34]

What a lesson Griz and Cat offer! We can help each other break free from the patterns of our past that keep us from loving each other. As we pray for and care for others with the love of Jesus Christ, we obtain healing by the grace of God, both for them and ourselves!

Never cease loving a person, and never give up hope for him; for even the Prodigal Son who had fallen most low could still be saved.

> The bitterest enemy and also he who was your friend could again be your friend; love that has grown cold can kindle again.
>
> SØREN AABYE KIERKEGAARD

UNDER WATER

Taking some time alone is a wonderful way to regroup, rethink, and refresh. It is needed at the time of day when we are a bit frayed from the day's activities, but the activities are not yet at an end. Unfortunately, not all of us can stop for a real break, but without this break, the remaining tasks may threaten to take us "under."

As the shadows of the day grow longer, our tempers can grow short. Drawing on the refreshing power of the Holy Spirit, however, will get us to the end of a stressful day. We can gain renewed patience, a fresh sense of humor, and a new surge of creativity and insight by enlisting the aid of the Spirit's ministry within us. Frequently it's during those late afternoon hours when we most need His extra help.

He knoweth the way that I take: when he hath tried me, I shall come forth as gold.

JOB 23:10 KJV

Jewelers claim that one of the surest tests for diamonds is the underwater test. "An imitation diamond is never so brilliant as a genuine stone. If your eye is not experienced to detect the difference, a simple test is to place the stone under water. The imitation diamond is practically extinguished, while a genuine diamond sparkles even under water and is distinctly visible. If a genuine stone is placed beside an imitation one under water, the contrast will be apparent to the least experienced eye."

That is how it should be with the Christian when his head is "under water" at the end of the day. The power of the Holy Spirit can so sparkle within him, refreshing and renewing him in spite of the day's harassments, that it is easy for the average person to tell there is something genuinely different about his life.

Ask the Holy Spirit to impart His power and presence to you today, in this very hour. Pray for Him to help you in the ways you need Him most—to shine like a diamond under water!

Breathe on me, breath of God;
Fill me with life anew,
That I may love what thou dost love,
And do what thou wouldst do.

EDWIN HATCH

THE SYMPATHETIC JEWEL

I say unto you, Love your enemies,
bless them that curse you, do good
to them that hate you, and pray for
them which despitefully use you,
and persecute you.

MATTHEW 5:44 KJV

Have you ever noticed that those who reject you often seem to lack joy. They could be guarded and standoffish because they have been rejected themselves. Their rejection of you may be a defense mechanism.

Sometimes your warm attitude toward them can make all the difference. This is illustrated by the story of a man who visited a jewelry store owned by a friend. His friend showed him magnificent diamonds and other splendid stones. Among these stones the visitor spotted one that seemed quite lusterless. Pointing to it, he said, "That stone has no beauty at all."

His friend put the gem in the hollow of his hand and closed his fingers tightly around it. In a few moments, he uncurled his fingers.

What a surprise! The entire stone gleamed with the splendor of a rainbow. "What have you done to it?" asked the astonished man.

His friend answered, "This is an opal. It is what we call the sympathetic jewel. It only needs to be gripped with the human hand to bring out its full beauty."

People are very much like opals. Without warmth, they become dull and colorless. But "grasp" them with the warmth and love of God, and they come alive with personality and humor. Unlike chameleons who simply adapt to their background, people who feel embraced by the love of God and His people come alive with colorful personalities all their own.

It's difficult to embrace those who have rejected us. However, if we can see beyond the facade they have erected to the potential inside them, we can be the healing hands of Jesus extended to them—and bring healing to ourselves in the process.

Men who walk in the ways of God would not grieve the hearts even of their enemies.

SA'DI

HELP OTHERS, HELP YOURSELF

A tornado rips through a southern town and destroys most of the buildings in its path. Those that remain standing have sustained serious damage, but the owners can't make all of the repairs.

A church in the South has a small congregation and an even smaller budget. Expenses are met each week, but the funds aren't there to hire someone to do minor but much-needed repairs.

Who comes to the rescue? A group of mostly retirees in recreational vehicles. They travel throughout the South during the autumn and winter months, escaping cold temperatures and doing good along the way. Some are experienced in carpentry and construction and some are not, but they all have the same goal: to make their time count by helping others.

> As the body without the spirit is dead, so faith without works is dead also.
>
> JAMES 2:26 KJV

The United Methodist Church chooses projects and assigns teams to each site. The workers, who pay all their expenses, meet at the appointed time and get right to work. To keep the jobs enjoyable, everyone works four days and then has three days off to relax and see the sights. The fun part, reported one female volunteer, is the opportunity to have fellowship with like-minded people.[35]

The same generosity of spirit, on a slightly different scale, is described in the Book of Acts. "All the believers were one in heart and mind. No one claimed that any of his possessions was his own, but they shared everything they had. There were no needy persons among them. For from time to time, those who owned lands or houses sold them, brought the money from the sales and put it at the apostles' feet, and it was distributed to anyone as he had need" (Acts 4:32, 34-35).

When we have the chance to do good, we should jump at it. "So in everything, do to others what you would have them do to you, for this sums up the Law and the Prophets," Jesus said in Matthew 7:12. Jesus asked us to serve, and we will be blessed when we do so.

Charity is never lost. It may meet with ingratitude, or be of no service to those on whom it was bestowed, yet it ever does a work of beauty and grace upon the heart of the giver.

CONYERS MIDDLETON

HIPPOS

When we think of a hippopotamus, the word "graceful" rarely comes to mind. Rather, we are likely to think of the words "cumbersome," "ugly," and "distorted." There is little to admire in the way a hippo looks or acts—or so we think. They seem to be large, rocklike masses, ready to tip over any unsuspecting boat that may pass too close.

Visitors to a new exhibit at a popular zoo are learning otherwise, however. A large glass aquarium gives visitors an opportunity to watch hippos from a different vantage point—under water.

They are surprised to discover that even with its short fat legs, bulky body, and oversized head, the hippopotamus is a very graceful, agile, and strong swimmer, capable of staying under water for long periods of time. The tiny eyes of the hippo are better adapted to the underwater murkiness of African rivers than to bright sunlight. Indeed, the hippo spends much of its time foraging along the bottoms of rivers.

> Then God saw everything that He had made, and indeed it was very good.
>
> GENESIS 1:31 NKJV

The main function of the hippo in the natural order appears to be that of "channel clearer."

Hippos eat enormous amounts of river grasses that grow along the banks of rivers, thus keeping the river free of blockages that might cause floods.

Ugly? Yes. But hippos are gifted in unusual ways and have a valuable role to play.

Every day you will encounter people who may seem awkward, different, ugly, or without much purpose. Look again! God has created each element of nature— plant, mineral, bird, fish, and animal—to fulfill a specific purpose and to do so with unique talents and abilities. There is an element of beauty, gracefulness, and goodness in everything He creates.

Everywhere I find the signature, the autograph of God.

JOSEPH PARKER

THE MIRACLE OF
A KIND WORD

Thou hast lifted me up, and hast not
made my foes to rejoice over me.

PSALM 30:1 KJV

The Reverend Purnell Bailey tells of a convict from Darlington, England, who had just been released from prison. He had spent three long years in prison for embezzlement, and though he wanted to return to his hometown, he was concerned about the social ostracism and possible ridicule he might have to endure from some of the townsfolk. Still, he was lonesome for his home and decided to risk the worst.

He had barely set foot on the main street of town when he encountered the mayor himself.

"Hello!" greeted the mayor in a cheery voice. "I'm glad to see you! How are you?" The man appeared ill at ease, so the mayor moved on.

Years later, the former mayor and the ex-convict accidentally met in another town. The latter said, "I want you to know what you did for me when I came out of prison."

"What did I do?" asked the mayor.

"You spoke a kind word to me and changed my life," replied the grateful man.[36]

We cannot always know how important the seed of a kind word may be to the one who receives it. More often than we know, words of encouragement or recognition provide a turning point in a person's outlook on life.

Just as Jesus spoke with love and acceptance to the hated tax collector Zaccheus, the mayor set the tone for others' contacts with the ex-convict by openly and warmly addressing him as a neighbor. People watch those they respect for cues regarding their own relationships with certain people.

Genuine, kind words cost the giver nothing but can mean the world to the one receiving them.

Today, don't be put off when someone to whom you offer a kind word seems uncomfortable or embarrassed. Recognize they may be unpracticed at receiving your love and compassion, even though they need it greatly.

Be kind; everyone you meet
is fighting a hard battle.

IAN MACLAREN

WHICH WAY IS UP?

Some years ago a speedboat driver described a harrowing racing accident from which he managed to survive. He had been nearing top speed when his boat veered slightly, striking a wave at a perilous angle. The combined force of his speed and the size and angle of the wave sent the boat flying into the air in a dangerous spin.

The driver was thrown out of his seat and propelled deep into the water—so deep, he had no idea which direction was "up." He had to remain calm and wait for the buoyancy of his life vest to begin pulling him toward the surface to know where the surface was. Then he swam quickly in that direction.

I will never leave you nor forsake you.

HEBREWS 13:5 NRSV

Life can put us in a tailspin at times, making us wonder, Which way is up? We can lose our sense of direction and the focus which keeps us on course. How do we recover our bearings?

The answer may be as simple as that discovered by the speedboat driver: Stay calm and let the "upward pull" bring you to the surface. The upward pull in our lives is that which looks beyond our finite selves to the greater reality of God.

A grandfather was taking a walk with his young granddaughter. He asked the little girl, "How far are we from home?"

The young girl answered, "Grandfather, I don't know."

"Well, do you know where you are?"

Again, seemingly unconcerned, "No, I don't know."

Then the grandfather said to her in his gentle, humorous way, "Sounds to me, honey, as if you are lost."

She looked up and said, "No, Grandfather, I can't be lost. I'm with you."

Our Heavenly Father never loses sight of us and never leaves us. As long as we remain aware of His presence and are sensitive to His "upward pull," we will always know which way is up!

Behind the dim unknown
standeth God within the shadow,
keeping watch above his own.

JAMES RUSSELL LOWELL

BEST FRIENDS

A student working on her doctoral thesis spent a year on a reservation in the Southwest living with a group of Navajo Indians. As the student did her research, she became part of a Native American family. She slept in their home, ate their food, worked with them, and generally lived their lifestyle.

The grandmother in the family did not speak English, yet she and the student were able to form a close bond of friendship. They spent much time together, forging a relationship that was meaningful to each one, yet difficult to explain to anyone else. The two shared experiences together even though they could not talk with each other. In spite of the language difference, they came to a closeness and mutual understanding and affection.

Over the months each one of them worked to learn phrases in the other one's language. The student learned some Navajo phrases, and the old grandmother picked up some English words.

When the year ended, it was time for the student to return to campus to write her thesis. The tribe held a going-away celebration

You were called into the fellowship of his Son, Jesus Christ our Lord.

1 CORINTHIANS 1:9 NRSV

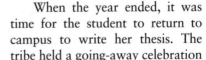

240

in honor of her stay and their friendship. The celebration was a sad occasion, because the young woman had become close to the entire village; she would miss them, and they would miss her.

As the student climbed into her pickup truck to leave, her dear friend, the old grandmother, came to say good-bye. With tears flowing down her cheeks, the grandmother put her hands on either side of the student's face. She looked directly into the young woman's eyes and said in her newly-learned words: "I like me best when I'm with you."

Good friends are the ones around whom we "like ourselves best" because they have a way of bringing out the best in us. Jesus is that kind of Friend to us. We can share all of our lives with Him, and He still accepts us with His great love. He will bring out the best in us, so we can say to Him, "I like me best when I'm with You."

There are some men and women in whose company we are always at our best.

All the best stops in our nature are drawn out, and we find a music in our souls never felt before.

WILLIAM HENRY DRUMMOND

SWEET REVENGE?

If thine enemy hunger, feed him;
if he thirst, give him drink: for in so
doing thou shalt heap coals of fire
on his head. Be not overcome of
evil, but overcome evil with good.

ROMANS 12:20-21 KJV

A young and hot-tempered officer in the Army struck a foot soldier. The foot soldier was also young and noted for his courage. He felt the insult deeply, but military discipline forbade him to return the blow. He said with conviction, however, "I will make you repent it."

One day in the heat of battle, the foot soldier saw an officer who was wounded and separated from his company. He gallantly forced his way through enemy lines to the officer, whom he recognized as the one who had insulted him. Nevertheless, he supported the wounded man with one arm as the two fought their way back to their own lines.

Trembling with emotion, the officer grasped the hand of the soldier and stammered out his gratitude, "Noble man! What a return for an insult so carelessly given!"

The young man pressed his hand in turn and with a smile said gently, "I told you I would make you repent it." From that time on they were as brothers.

John Wesley found another positive and helpful way to settle quarrels. In his journal he wrote of a disagreement that took place in one of the religious gatherings called Societies. Fourteen people were expelled from the group as a result. Not seeing any good reason why such an action should have taken place, Wesley called the entire group together to try to bring about reconciliation.

Prior to the sermon, prayer, and communion, Wesley recalls, "I willingly received them all again; requiring only one condition of the contenders on both sides, to say not one word of anything that was past." He then goes on to describe the healing that took place in the group when the recounting of old wounds was eliminated as a possibility.

Extending God's grace to those who have wronged us can repair just about any broken relationship. Instead of returning anger with anger, kindness proves the best peacemaker.

By taking revenge, a man is but even with his enemy; but in passing over it, he is superior.

FRANCIS BACON

OPEN THE DOOR

A nurse on duty in a pediatric ward often gave the children an opportunity to listen to their own hearts with her stethoscope. One day she put the stethoscope into a little boy's ears. She asked him, "Can you hear that? What do you suppose that is?"

The little boy frowned a moment, caught up in the wonder of this strange tapping inside his chest. Then he broke into a grin and responded, "Is that Jesus knocking?"

> Behold, I stand at the door, and knock: if any man hear my voice, and open the door, I will come in to him, and will sup with him, and he with me.
>
> REVELATION 3:20 KJV

Another story is told of a group of students who went to visit a great religious teacher. The wise teacher asked the young scholars a seemingly obvious question. "Where is the dwelling place of God?"

The students laughed among themselves and replied, "What a thing to ask! Is not the whole world full of His glory?"

The learned old man smiled and replied, "God dwells wherever man lets Him in."

The little boy listening to his heart through the stethoscope seemed to have more wisdom than the group of students. With his innocent, trusting faith, he had no problem believing that Jesus was knocking on his heart's door.

Imagine your life to be a house of many rooms. Each room represents a different aspect of your life. Some of the rooms are messed up, others are clean and tidy. The doors that are locked represent areas where you have not invited Jesus to enter.

Like the little boy, when we hear Jesus knocking at the closed doors of our lives, it is up to us to open the door and let Him in. Even those rooms that are dark and frightening are filled with light and understanding when Jesus enters.

You need not cry very loud;
he is nearer to us than we think.

BROTHER LAWRENCE OF THE RESURRECTION

BE YOURSELF!

A father tells of his young daughter who, like many American girls, had a large collection of dolls. Modern dolls, he noted, are far different from their predecessors. Today a girl has a choice of owning a doll that can "walk and talk, drink and wink, slurp, burp, cry, sigh, and laugh"—almost anything a real baby does, including wet itself and even get diaper rash.

After years of buying the most modern dolls for his daughter, the man wondered which of these marvels was her favorite. To his surprise, he found she especially liked the small rag doll she had been given on her third birthday.

The novelty of all the other performing dolls had long worn off, but this simple rag doll had allowed her to love it. The other dolls had caught her eye, but the rag doll had won her heart.

> The LORD looks on the heart.
>
> 1 SAMUEL 16:7 NRSV

To his little girl, the rag doll was real and was loved just the way it was—missing both eyes and most of its hair. After all the years and lost parts, the doll was still what it had always been—just itself.

Too often, we are like the high-tech dolls. We try to impress others with our skills, talent, education, specch, or other abilities, when what we need to do is simply be ourselves.

Within every person lies the innate desire to be loved, accepted, and pleasing to others. But if we spend all our energy trying to be something we are not, we will never know the joy of being loved for who we are.

Be yourself! Genuine love is not a reward for performance or achievement. People may like or admire you for what you can do, but they will love you for who you are.

Likewise, try to see past others' performances or efforts to gain attention or approval. Try to look past exteriors and outer appearances that may betray the true condition of the heart. Love others for who they are.

> We are so accustomed to wearing
> a disguise before others that we
> are unable to recognize ourselves.
>
> FRANÇOIS DUC DE LA ROCHEFOUCAULD

BE A BLESSING COUNTER

> I will bless them and the places surrounding my hill. I will send down showers in season; there will be showers of blessing.
>
> EZEKIEL 34:26

"Oh no, not again," Wendy whispered to herself, as she awoke from a sound sleep at exactly two o'clock in the morning. For several nights now, she had awakened in the middle of the night, unable to get back to sleep.

Wendy tried counting sheep forward and backward, but she remained wide awake. Warm milk only served to make her more alert. For several hours each night, she made herself miserable, trying to force herself to go back to sleep and worrying about the cause of her problem.

During the day, she found it hard to focus on her studies, and the dark rings under her eyes made her look and feel even worse.

The next time she awoke during the early morning hours, Wendy picked up her Bible and began to read and study the Scriptures. For many nights to follow, she searched God's Word, while gradually understanding the message it offered. Her sheep counting changed to blessing counting, and she discovered quickly that she always fell asleep before she could count them all.

Instead of dreading her insomnia, she now looked forward to studying God's Word in the middle of the night. His power and presence filled her soul. Gradually, the more time she spent with God, the more she gained spiritual power and an increased feeling of self-worth. For the first time in a long time, she felt in control of her feelings and began to believe that with Him she could do all things.

Eventually, Wendy's insomnia faded away, and her sleep grew sweet. She made sure, however, that she spent time alone with God during the day. But still she is grateful for the sleepless nights; God used that time to teach her the truth of living and the joy of loving. She learned, as she counted her blessings, that the answer to peaceful sleep is not in counting sheep but in calling on the Shepherd.

Reflect upon your present blessings of which every man has many; not on your past misfortunes of which all men have some.

CHARLES DICKENS

GOD'S MASTERPIECE

French painter Claude Monet painted the world in a new way. In one of his most famous works, Impression: Sunrise, Monet used only color to create a composition. With no outlines, shapes were only suggested and blurred. His purpose was to catch a fleeting moment; moments later, the sun would be in another position, the small boat would have moved, and all would look different.

> Now we see through a glass, darkly; but then face to face: now I know in part; but then shall I know even as also I am known.
>
> 1 CORINTHIANS 13:12 KJV

Working outdoors, Monet painted landscapes directly from nature. He had to work quickly, before the light changed, leaving little time to worry about fine detail. He wanted to catch just a glimpse of a particular moment in time. The altering light allowed him to see the same object in different ways. Monet often painted a series of paintings of the same subject to show these different appearances as the light changed.[37]

God's radiant light shapes our perspective of life. While we may not fully understand why we go through difficulties or changes in our lives, the struggles we face on earth are fleeting moments compared to spending eternity with God. Difficult situations can sometimes blur our ability to see God's best for us, because we are seeing only a small glimpse of what God is doing.

Staring at the unfinished canvas of our lives, we tend to miss the beauty of the masterpiece in progress. We may see only splashes of color without form or reason, never stepping back to visualize the entire spectrum of experiences that brought us to this point in our lives.

Spend time in God's illuminating presence. It will refresh your outlook and give you a different way of looking at life's daily problems, as the Master completes the composition within you.

It isn't your problems that are bothering you. It is the way you are looking at them.

EPICTETUS

PILLARS OF STONE

Hidden beneath the Chihuahuan Desert in New Mexico lies one of God's great wonders, Carlsbad Caverns. To the casual visitor, its dark entrance can seem uninteresting, like the surrounding barren desert itself. Yet here is subtlety and grandeur, where over the centuries tiny drops of water, silently in the dark, built a startlingly beautiful monument forty feet high. Drop after drop, depositing particle after particle, a marble-like finger begins to grow. Ultimately, this process forms a tremendous pillar; thus, the cavern's sculptures are created.[38]

A similar process goes on inside each of us. As a single thought finds its way into our minds, it leaves sediment that sinks deep down within our souls, forming our own pillars—pillars of character. If we let immoral, selfish, and violent thoughts fill our minds, we form eroding pillars of evil and failure. If we fill our

Finally, beloved, whatever is true, whatever is honorable, whatever is just, whatever is pure, whatever is pleasing, whatever is commendable, if there is any excellence and if there is anything worthy of praise, think about these things.

PHILIPPIANS 4:8 NRSV

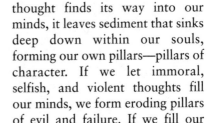

252

minds with truth and love, we form strong and beautiful pillars within our souls.

In Proverbs 23:7 (KJV), King Solomon said, "For as he thinketh in his heart, so is he." Solomon understood that the things we dwell on determine the person we become. When we pursue God, we begin to reflect His character in our lives.

What formed the pillars of character in your life? Do you bear any resemblance to your Heavenly Father?

You can become the person God has designed you to be by renewing your mind daily in the Word of God. Just as the Carlsbad Caverns were developed over time, hidden from view, so our own true character is built.

The mind grows by what it feeds on.

JOSIAH GILBERT HOLLAND

RUMINATING ON GOD'S WORD

This Book of the Law shall not depart from your mouth, but you shall meditate in it day and night, that you may observe to do according to all that is written in it.

JOSHUA 1:8 NKJV

Have you ever watched the news before going to bed and then dreamed about one of the news stories on the broadcast? The last thing we think about just before we doze off settles deep within our subconscious mind. Like clothes in a washing machine on the spin cycle, thoughts spin around all night in our minds. Then they often return to our consciousness as the first thought we have in the morning.

King David said in Psalm 4:4 (NKJV), "Meditate within your heart on your bed and be still." Before you fall asleep, think about God's Word and what God is doing in your life. Ask yourself, what is the condition of my spirit? Am I fulfilling God's plan for my life? That will not only deepen your relationship with God, it also will expand your knowledge of Him.

Meditate—or ruminate—on God's Word as you lie on your bed at night. To ruminate, as defined by Webster's dictionary, means "to go over in the mind repeatedly and often casually or slowly." By spending time going over and over a Scripture, you can draw from it the depth of its meaning. The Bible reminds us to be transformed by the renewing of the mind.

So before retiring for the night, read a passage or two of Scripture. As you drift off to sleep, meditate on it. When you wake, you will have "ruminated" all night on God's Word, waking refreshed and renewed. Then in the morning, you can praise God as King David did: "My voice You shall hear in the morning, O LORD; In the morning I will direct it to You, and I will look up" (Psalm 5:3 NKJV).

Think often on God, by day, by night, in your business, and even in your diversions. He is always near you and with you; leave him not alone. You would think it rude to leave a friend alone who came to visit you; why, then, must God be neglected?

BROTHER LAWRENCE OF

THE RESURRECTION

Ships in the Night

As Rebecca's one-year-old son, Dylan, played in the bathtub with his favorite toy—a little sailor—she silently asked God how they should spend the rest of the day. Every day seemed to be the same, a combination of errands and housework.

Dylan grabbed the sailor and plopped him in his boat, splashing water in Rebecca's face. Somehow, the splashing water reminded her that Navy ships had recently docked in their port city. There are men in those ships! she mused.

> God hath given thee all them that sail with thee.
>
> Acts 27:24 KJV

Rebecca's family always enjoyed visiting the Navy vessels, but this time she sensed God directing her family to minister to the six hundred servicemen who had been at sea for the last five months. But how? Rebecca grabbed a towel and her dripping-wet baby and took off to go shopping for the newly arrived sailors.

As night drew near, Rebecca and the rest of her family climbed aboard a guided missile destroyer carrying gifts. The sailors, eager to see what was inside the green and gold boxes, greeted them. After the command duty officer was summoned on deck to receive their gifts, the officer offered to take Rebecca's family on a private tour.

To their surprise, when they visited the wardroom, they saw that one of the boxes had already been placed at the head of the captain's table. Trying not to notice, Rebecca quickly looked away, staring at a portrait. In the reflection of the glass, she watched an officer take something out of the box. She sensed the Lord whispering to her, I want them all, so I start at the top.

Lightly touching the rails, Rebecca's family prayed for each man who would hold that rail during the stormy seas of life. As the sailors lowered the American flag and illuminated the friendship lights, Rebecca's family bid them farewell.

Tonight, ask the Lord how He wants you to spend your tomorrow. Be available for Him. In doing so, you may touch many lives and make new friends.

> You never know till you try to reach them how accessible men are; but you must approach each man by the right door.
>
> HENRY WARD BEECHER

SOLDIER OF THE CROSS

Joseph, a seventeen-year-old patriot of the American Revolution, clutched his musket to his chest and leaned into the bitter wind. Exhausted, his eyes half-shut against the cold, he slipped on an icy rut. Valley Forge was twelve miles away; he realized the Army had a long and painful march ahead of them.

This is how he described the circumstances:

> We were literally starved. I did not put a morsel of victuals into my mouth for four days and as many nights, except a little black-birch bark which I gnawed off a stick of wood. I saw several of the men roast their old shoes and eat them. The Army is now not only starved but naked. The greatest part were not only shirtless and barefoot, but destitute of all other clothing, especially blankets. . . . Hundreds of my companions had to go barefoot, till they could be tracked by their blood upon the rough frozen ground.[39]

Fight the good fight of faith.

1 TIMOTHY 6:12 KJV

The last few miles to Valley Forge were uphill, and the weary soldiers struggled to keep going. Because of the lack of supplies and the barrenness of the surrounding countryside, the men were without adequate shelter, food, or clothing; they lived in crude huts built by their own hands. Many died of starvation and cold. This was one of the darkest periods of the American Revolution. Yet it was at Valley Forge in February, 1778, that the Army was trained, disciplined, and reorganized. And despite all the hardships they suffered, these soldiers continued the fight for America's independence.

How many of us today would endure such extreme hardships for our beliefs? During hard times, we are trained and disciplined to endure the stresses of life and appreciate the blessings of God. Tonight, ask God for the stamina to help lead others to the kind of freedom that can only be found in Christ.

> Adversities do not make a man frail;
> they show what sort of man he is.
>
> THOMAS A KEMPIS

THE WHITE CANE

Rise in the presence of the aged,
show respect for the elderly and
revere your God. I am the LORD.

LEVITICUS 19:32

The first time Cathi saw Hank, a cantankerous old man, he was leaning over the receptionist's desk with his white cane raised high and yelling at the top of his lungs. Part of Cathi's job as a student volunteer for the state's social services division was to visit elderly residents in their homes with their caseworker, but Hank couldn't wait. He was letting the whole office know about his problems.

Hank no doubt had been tall and robust before age took its toll on his body. His eighty-year-old body might have shrunk in stature, but his mind was still sharp; and Cathi was just another thorn in his side.

Unsure of the reception they would receive, she was filled with trepidation the first time she accompanied the caseworker to Hank's house. He acted out with his usual yelling and cane-waving, probably just to see how fast they would run. Slowly Cathi began to detect an undercurrent of sadness in the old man. Hank had out-lived all his family and friends, including his wife. They had no children. Cathi thought of how lonely life must be for Hank. Maybe his cane-waving was a bid for attention, the way a two-year-old throws a temper tantrum for the same reason.

Over the course of the next year, Cathi and the case-worker visited Hank many times. They found him to be an intelligent man whose body had just gotten too old for him; he simply couldn't do the things he wanted to do.

We have much to learn from the elderly; they form a bridge from the past to the present and to the future. Do you have a "Hank" in your family or neighbor-hood? That person may suffer from loneliness, just as Hank did.

Nothing is more beautiful than cheerfulness in an old face.

JOHANN PAUL FRIEDRICH RICHTER

FOOTPRINTS

John loved to run and walk in the park during the mild winter weather where he lived. So he was surprised one morning in mid-January when he discovered that the area had been covered with a blanket of snow during the night. But since he was up early anyway, John decided to go ahead and run on the graveled jogging trail in the park. No one had been out yet to leave footprints in the snow, but he had been on the trail often enough to know its general direction and its twists and turns. John forged a path along the trail, leaving the prints of his shoes in the snow. After several laps, other joggers joined him on the course, following in his footprints.

> Lift your drooping hands and strengthen your weak knees, and make straight paths for your feet.
>
> HEBREWS 12:12-13 NRSV

Later that day, John returned to the park to walk his dogs. As he walked around the jogging trail, he noticed that the melting snow showed the route of the graveled trail in many places. It differed from the path of footprints. Now that the path was partially visible, people followed it rather than the footprints in the snow.

John thought about the way he lived his life. Most individuals follow an established way rather than forging their own path. It is a unique person who breaks away and makes his own footsteps. Did he know God's pathway well enough to walk in it when faced with uncertain circumstances? Did he set a course so that those who followed him would not be misled?

Tonight, ask yourself whether you know God's path for your life. All of us have doubts as we go through life, but if we study God's Word and keep our eyes on Jesus, we can follow in the footsteps of our faith. We can make footprints for those who come after us.[40]

God made the moon as well as the sun; and when he does not see fit to grant us the sunlight, he means us to guide our steps by moonlight.

RICHARD WHATELY

A MICROWAVE FRIEND

When Sara was a little girl and went to visit her grandpa, he would set her on the kitchen counter and let her watch him make popcorn in the popcorn machine. Those special times with Grandpa and the popcorn machine were not to last. The problem was not that Sara had grown too big to sit on the counter. Rather, Grandpa discovered the convenience of microwave popcorn. It was easy, cheap, and quick.

Now when Sara visits him, Grandpa asks her to put a bag into the "micro" and "nuke" it. Sara eats the popcorn, but she looks around the kitchen and there's no Grandpa enjoying it with her. It only takes one person to stick a bag of popcorn into the microwave. Sara misses those precious moments of making popcorn with him.

> There are "friends" who pretend to be friends, but there is a friend who sticks closer than a brother.
>
> PROVERBS 18:24 TLB

Have we become a generation of microwave friends—friends who are here one minute and gone the next, like a fast-food hamburger? We used to call this type of friend an acquaintance—someone we meet occasionally in our daily lives—someone to have lunch with, meet at the same party, or see a movie with once in a while. It is enjoyable sharing our time with these people, but we know they are not the friends who would sacrifice themselves to help us in a time of need.

The individual we can count on to assist us and whom we would sacrifice our needs to help in any and all circumstances is our true friend. This is the person we have spent time with, cried with, and rejoiced with—the person we have a history with and have taken the time to discover who and what he or she is like and what this friend believes in. A person who shares the same belief system we do. Friendship is a relationship that stays strong no matter what.

God made us to need one another. Cultivate real friendships and weed out the phony ones.[41]

Real friendship is shown in times of trouble; prosperity is full of friends.

EURIPIDES

BEAR IN THE CAVE

"My command is this: Love
each other as I have loved you.
Greater love has no one than this, that
he lay down his life for his friends."

JOHN 15:12-13

An old story tells the tale of two teenage boys who were cave exploring when they found what appeared to be huge bear tracks deep inside a long, cavernous tunnel. They decided to keep moving into the pitch-black cave but crept ahead slowly and with extreme caution. Shining their flashlights into every dark crevice, they kept their eyes and ears open in case they actually encountered a bear.

Suddenly from behind a rock jumped the meanest looking grizzly bear they had ever seen. Standing up in front of them, the bear roared like a lion, sending a terrible sound echoing off the walls of the cave. The two scared boys scrambled back toward the front of the cave with the bear roaring behind them. Then one of the boys dropped to the floor, quickly untied his hiking boots, whipped them off, and jammed on his running shoes.

His friend yelled at him, "Come on, man! Let's get out of here! Why in the world are you changing shoes? We don't have much of a chance of outrunning that bear anyway!"

Lunging to his feet and starting to run, the first boy replied, "I don't have to outrun the bear. All I have to do is outrun you."

Jesus said in the Bible that a friend is one who will give up his life for you, just as He did for all of us. But a fair-weather friend is one who will only be there for you as long as there's no risk involved. What kind of friend are you?[42]

The friendship that can cease has never been real.

SAINT JEROME

THE TARNISHED CUP

After hours of searching through dusty cartons in the basement, brushing aside spider webs and dust bunnies, Kelly found the box that contained the baby cup that had been her grandmother's. It was wrapped in yellowed newspaper from many years earlier, as evidenced by the dates on the paper. Kelly removed the wrapping and discovered that the cup was now blackened by tarnish. Frustrated and disappointed, she stuffed the cup back into the carton.

That night Kelly was unable to sleep. After an hour of tossing and turning, it finally occurred to her that she was uneasy because her neglect and lack of concern had allowed the cup to deteriorate. She got up quickly and retrieved the cup from the basement. Finding some silver polish, she gently cleaned the cup until the beautiful silver again was revealed. With much work and love, she restored the cup to its original beauty.

Often our relationships with family and friends tarnish and

> Stop being mean, bad-tempered and angry. Quarreling, harsh words, and dislike of others should have no place in your lives. Instead, be kind to each other, tenderhearted, forgiving one another, just as God has forgiven you because you belong to Christ.
>
> EPHESIANS 4:31-32 TLB

deteriorate under layers of hurt feelings, anger, and mis-understanding. Sometimes the deterioration begins with a comment made in the heat of the moment, or it may begin under the strain of other stresses. If the air isn't cleared immediately, the relationship tarnishes.

When we put work and love into our relationships, they can be restored. Then we rediscover the beauty that lies underneath the tarnish and realize that it has been there all along.

If you're lying awake tonight, unable to sleep because you've been hurt by a loved one or you've said hurtful words or retaliated in kind, remember the teachings of Jesus and ask forgiveness for yourself and your loved one.[43]

If men would consider not so much wherein they differ, as wherein they agree, there would be far less uncharitableness and angry feeling in the world.

JOSEPH ADDISON

FIERY TRIALS

On the slopes of the rugged Sierra Nevada, the giant sequoias inhabit a forest realm that they have ruled for millennia. From the mists of the ancient past they have emerged—the largest of all living things on earth—a symbol of an incredible will to survive.

> The fire will test each one's work, of what sort it is. If anyone's work which he has built on it endures, he will receive a reward. If anyone's work is burned, he will suffer loss; but he himself will be saved, yet so as through fire.
>
> 1 CORINTHIANS 3:13-15 NKJV

Over the thousands of years the sequoia have existed, they have had to make changes in order to endure. The most important of these adaptations has to do with fire, since lightning storms are common in the foothills of the forest.

These trees have developed a thick, fire-resistant bark, which burns poorly and protects them from the intense heat generated by fires. Although a particularly hot fire may succeed in burning a tree and leaving a scar, a healing process begins almost immediately. New bark creeps over the wounds until the breach is covered and fully protected again.

Natural fires also provide optimum conditions for germination.

Hot updrafts dry and open old cones, releasing seeds that shower the forest floor. The freshly burned floor, now cleared of undergrowth and competing trees, allows the seedlings access to sunlight and minerals in the soil.[44]

The fires, or trials of life, that we endure also help to burn away the undergrowth and weeds of our faults that prevent us from growing and maturing in the Lord. Weeds such as greed, pride, and ungratefulness must be removed in order for us to bear fruit in our lives.

Just as the seedlings need sunlight and minerals to survive, we thrive on God's light by entering His presence through prayer and receive nourishment by reading His Word daily. Although the trials of life are painful to bear, God is there to begin the healing process and fully protect us during those times.

Afflictions make the heart more deep, more experimental, more knowing and profound, and so, more able to hold, to contain, and beat more.

JOHN BUNYAN

OUT OF THE SPOTLIGHT

His anger is but for a moment;
his favor is for a lifetime.
Weeping may linger for the night,
but joy comes with the morning.

PSALM 30:5 NRSV

As a teenager, LuAnne entered a national beauty pageant. She'd won several other beauty contests; she was blessed with beautiful, long-brown hair, dark-brown eyes, a trim figure, a sense of humor, and a natural intelligence. This was the first time, however, that she would compete nationally.

More than anything, LuAnne wanted to win the pageant. She figured taking home a national title would boost her self-esteem and that it would eliminate all her problems—at least most of them.

The night of the contest, LuAnne carefully applied her make-up and slipped into a long, flowing, pink chiffon evening gown. On stage, she smiled widely and walked with elegance. For the talent portion, she sang better than ever.

Later, the announcer read, "And the winner is LuAnne . . . " The applause roared in her ears. She was so thrilled. Finally, she thought, I'm somebody!

But when LuAnne returned home, she soon realized that she still had problems just like everyone else. In fact, her life was filled with more stress than before the contest. She traveled around the country giving speeches while trying to maintain high academic grades. In addition, she had to meet deadlines for television and newspaper interviews.

After months and months of a hectic schedule, LuAnne felt drained of all energy. She looked forward to the day when her reign as a beauty queen would end and a new girl would take her place. She wanted her old life back so that she could spend time with her friends.

Soon the year passed, and a new queen was selected for the upcoming year. LuAnne was more than happy to step out of the spotlight.

Our stress-filled problems may seem to offer no solutions, but there is hope. We can find joy and peace. We may have to struggle first through the night, but joy comes in the morning. That's one of God's promises. What a beautiful one!

Hope not only bears up the mind under sufferings but makes her rejoice in them.

JOSEPH ADDISON

ONLY THE BEST

When God sprinkled the stars across the universe, He knew exactly where He wanted to place each and every one. He took control of the gravitation of the earth, the tilt of its axis, and the orbit of the moon. Knowing exactly how much heat the world would need, He provided the sun and all its glory.

> God exalted him to the highest place and gave him the name that is above every name.
>
> PHILIPPIANS 2:9

God even thought of little things when He formed the universe. He knew that His children would enjoy snow sometimes and warm weather at other times. He knew that the joy of nature would bring peace and contentment to hearts and souls everywhere. God also thought of the fact that without friendship, His children could become lonely. He wanted only the best for His creation, so He planned out everything carefully.

He wanted to be sure that when the nights seemed too long and the days too short His children could continue to experience peace, so He provided many wonderful gifts along the way. The gift of salvation is the most wonderful present that could ever be offered or received. He provided the sacrifice in the form of a man—a perfect man, no less. His name was Jesus, the

Name above all names. He lived, died, and lives again; and that enables us to live forever.

Because He lives, beauty can be found in the darkness, just as it can be found during the daylight hours. Looking at the stars and seeing the glow of the moon can bring joy to the soul of man. Sleepless nights can become blessings if God's children use that time to seek His face.

The power of God can be magnificent in the quietness of the night. His presence can be felt in an uplifting way through prayer and worship. He is worthy of our praise, even when the night seems long. It's through the difficulties that we learn to trust the sweetest name on earth—Jesus.

O for a thousand tongues to sing
my great Redeemer's praise!

CHARLES WESLEY

HAVE YOU FORGIVEN?

One day Corrie ten Boom visited a friend in the hospital. Though her friend was quite ill, Corrie noticed that she also was quite bitter.

At first, the two women spent time catching up on each other's lives. Finally the woman said that her husband disliked having a sick wife, and as a result, he had left and was living with a younger woman. Knowing that her friend was greatly distressed, Corrie asked, "Have you forgiven him?"

The woman said, "Certainly not!"

At first Corrie had trouble believing that her friend had not forgiven her husband. Then she remembered a time when she herself had been unforgiving. After World War II, she had recognized a nurse who had been cruel to her dying sister while they were detained in the Ravensbruck concentration camp. The memories flooded back, and she recalled how her sister had suffered because of this nurse.

"If you do not forgive men their sins, your Father will not forgive your sins."

Matthew 6:15

In that moment, Corrie knew that she had not forgiven. She knew she must forgive, but she

276

couldn't seem to bring herself to do it. She finally had a talk with God.

"Lord," she said, "You know I cannot forgive her. My sister suffered too much because of her cruelties." The Lord revealed Romans 5:5 (KJV) to Corrie: "The love of God is shed abroad in our hearts by the Holy Ghost which is given unto us." Then she prayed, "Thank You, Father, that Your love in me is stronger than my bitterness."

When she finally met the nurse, Corrie told her that although she had been bitter about what happened to her sister, now she loved her. By the end of their conversation, Corrie shared the way to salvation, and the nurse accepted Jesus Christ as her Lord and Savior.[45]

Forgiving someone else is powerful. It is a blessing to the one forgiven, but it also releases the one forgiving from the bondage of bitterness. If you need to forgive someone today, ask God to show you how.

Life lived without forgiveness becomes a prison.

WILLIAM ARTHUR WARD

IN JESUS' NAME

My purpose is that they may be
encouraged in heart and united in love,
so that they may have the full riches of
complete understanding, in order that
they may know the mystery of God,
namely, Christ, in whom are hidden all
the treasures of wisdom and knowledge.

COLOSSIANS 2:2-3

Thirty-seven-year-old Joyce Girgenti, a Christian artist, shares her faith by painting the name of Jesus into her inspirational paintings.

One year, Joyce was approached by an organization who wanted her to donate a Christmas card scene. Her first effort, a fireplace scene complete with a Christmas tree and nativity, was turned down. Undaunted, Joyce replaced the scene with another, and it was accepted. Later, Joyce realized why her original scene was rejected; God had other plans.

Joyce had used a photo of her own fireplace to paint the original scene. Working from the top of the canvas, she painted the Christmas tree, the nativity on the mantel, the roaring fire, and the stones that formed the fireplace. As she began to paint the bottom of the fireplace, she turned to her daughter. "Wouldn't it be neat to hide something in the fireplace that refers to Christmas?" she asked.

Before her daughter could answer, Joyce said, "What better than Jesus? He's why we celebrate Christmas." She then arranged the fireplace stones to spell out the name of Jesus. At her daughter's urging, she added a stone that resembled a heart.

After her card was rejected, Joyce used it to send to clients and friends. One day, Joyce received a call from her friend, Mary, who asked, "Is Jesus' name really in your fireplace?" She had called to verify what she'd found.

In each of her inspirational paintings, Joyce seeks to please God by painting Jesus' name somewhere in her work. She shares her faith with everyone she meets, saying, "If you forget me, you've lost nothing, but if you forget Jesus, you've lost everything."

It's a mystery trying to find His name so well hidden in Joyce's paintings, but the real mystery is not His name—it's Jesus himself. Only when Jesus is revealed are we able to discern His hidden treasure for us—His gift of salvation.

Sin separates, pain isolates, but salvation and comfort unite.

JULIAN OF NORWICH

A Flash Prayer

Nan stood at the window one winter day watching the wind whipping the pine trees. The cold rain had sneaked in the night before. Early that morning, she had struggled to get out of bed as the extreme cold and dampness wreaked havoc on her joints.

At the post office, everyone seemed to feel as she did. No one smiled, and everyone seemed to be struggling through the day. She decided then and there to at least change her own outlook. She smiled—not a forced smile, but a caring smile that radiated the love of God. For some, she whispered a "flash prayer" that their day would be blessed by the Heavenly Father.

As she went about her day, her smiles brought blessings from God in the form of a grandmother who rushed to her side to share a funny story, a man who asked her opinion on which handbag to buy for his wife, and the boy who allowed her to take his place in the express lane.

Dear friends, since God so loved us, we also ought to love one another. No one has ever seen God; but if we love one another, God lives in us and his love is made complete in us.

1 John 4:11-12

Nan remembered how a smile began a friendship with a young grocery-store bagger with Downs syndrome. One winter day, with snow clouds slung low across the sky, the young man carried her groceries to her car. Digging in her purse for a tip, she was embarrassed when she found she had nothing to give him.

"I'm sorry," she said, not wanting to disappoint the young man.

A smile as bright as the summer sun spread across his face. "That's OK," he said. Then he wrapped his arms around her. "I love you," he said. Shivering in the cold, she whispered a "flash prayer" for this special child of God. "Lord, bless this precious child," she whispered.

Sometimes the most unexpected encounters can teach us a lesson in humility, but the greatest lesson in humility is found in Jesus Christ.[46] Tonight, whisper a "flash prayer" for someone you saw today.

As it is the business of tailors
to make clothes and of cobblers
to mend shoes, so it is the
business of Christians to pray.

MARTIN LUTHER

STARRY, STARRY NIGHT

Remember when you were a child, lying on your back outdoors, staring up at the celestial stream of stars and the moon? All was peaceful and still. How relaxing it was to quietly gaze at the shimmering lights and simply dream! Everyone needs a quiet time to be alone with God, without television or radio. If you can't find quiet time, it's because you've given it away. But you can take it back now.

You are more special than all the other things God created, even the stars in the heavens. The psalmist wrote in Psalm 8:3-5 (KJV), "When I consider thy heavens, the work of thy fingers, the moon and the stars, which thou hast ordained; What is man, that thou art mindful of him? And the son of man, that thou visitest him? For thou hast made him a little lower than the angels, and hast crowned him with glory and honour."

> The heavens declare the glory of God; and the firmament sheweth his handywork.
>
> PSALM 19:1 KJV

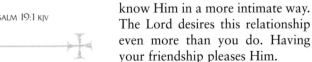

God has a special place in His heart just for you and wants you to know Him in a more intimate way. The Lord desires this relationship even more than you do. Having your friendship pleases Him.

Don't listen to the lies of the enemy, who tells you that God is angry because you haven't read your Bible lately. As you spend time with God, you will be strengthened. This strength will keep you from throwing in the towel when times get tough. Make your quiet time top priority. Consider it an appointment with God. Mark on your calendar now the time you plan to spend with God each day, and give it first place.

The Bible grows more beautiful as we grow in our understanding of it.

JOHANN WOLFGANG VON GOETHE

SOMETIMES
MIRACLES HIDE

I am greatly encouraged; in all our
troubles my joy knows no bounds.

2 CORINTHIANS 7·4

Charles Dickens' book A Christmas Carol has become one of the best-loved stories of all time. But few know that it grew out of one of the darkest periods in the author's career and changed his life forever.

At age thirty-one and at the peak of his career, Dickens was facing serious financial trouble. Unexpected news that his other novels were not selling well stunned the young man and resurfaced memories and insecurities of his childhood poverty. He supported a large extended family, and his wife was expecting their fifth child. What would he do?

After months of depression, Dickens was walking through the black streets of London where "bawdy streetwalkers, pickpockets, footpads, and beggars" roamed. The scene reminded him of a recurring nightmare: a twelve-year-old boy working twelve hours a day, six days a week, attaching labels on an endless stream of pots to earn the six shillings that would keep him alive. Sitting in that dingy, rat-infested warehouse, the boy saw that the light outside was fading, along with his hopes. His father was in debtors' prison, and the boy felt hopeless, abandoned.

The dream was a true scene from Dickens' childhood. Fortunately, his father inherited some money, paid his debts, and was released from prison.

Suddenly, Dickens knew he must write A Christmas Carol for those people he saw who could identify with his own fears. Strangely, with Scrooge's change of heart in the novel and Dickens' festive description of Christmas cheer and celebrations, Dickens' own depression faded. The much-loved book helped restore his confidence and paved the way to many more treasured stories.[47]

Like Dickens' experience, miracles often hide in the midst of self-doubt and confusion. Focusing on the joys of Christmas renews our hope in the season and restores our faith in what God can accomplish through us.

Reflect upon your present
blessings of which every man
has many; not on your past
misfortunes of which all
men have some.

CHARLES DICKENS

A PARTY FOR JESUS

How would you feel if a party was given in your honor, and the people attending gave presents to one another but not to you?

That's the question the youth pastor addressed at the group's weekend retreat. As the students settled into their seats, the youth pastor said, "We like to visit with one another, but from this point on, let's talk only about Jesus. He is our guest of honor this weekend."

As the students listened intently, the youth pastor led a conversation about Jesus. The focal point became a wooden cross.

> Today in the city of David there has been born for you a Savior, who is Christ the Lord.
>
> LUKE 2:11 NASB

The students discussed everything from Jesus' humble birth to His death on the cross and His glorious resurrection.

Then he announced, "Every party has gifts. Now it's time for us to give our gifts to Jesus." He passed around a basket filled with tiny, decorated boxes. At the appointed time, each student opened a box in an attitude of prayer and read aloud a Scripture, along with the companion "gift" to place on an altar. These included such things as:

- my heart
- my faith
- my future
- my dreams

During the touching, intimate moment, several students moved to a kneeling position and then wept softly. That day became special, because they chose to give Jesus the most meaningful gift of all: themselves.

> He who knows God
> reverences him.
>
> LUCIUS ANNAEUS SENECA

NOT WORTH A DIME

The story is told of a young man who was invited to preach at a church in Nashville, Tennessee. On an impulse he used as his text, "Thou shalt not steal."

The next morning he stepped onto a city bus and handed the driver a dollar bill. The driver handed him his change, and he walked to the rear of the bus to stand, since there were no seats available.

Once he had steadied himself, he counted his change. There was a dime too much. His first thought was, The bus company will never miss this dime.

By now the bus had stopped again, and the narrow aisle between him and the driver was one long line of people. Then it hit him; he could not keep money that did not belong to him.

A half dozen "excuse me's" and several scowling looks later, he made his way to the front and said to the driver, "You gave me too much change."

The driver replied, "Yes, a dime too much. I gave it to you on purpose. You see, I heard your

"There is nothing concealed that will not be disclosed, or hidden that will not be made known."

Luke 12:2

sermon yesterday, and I watched in my mirror as you counted your change. Had you kept the dime, I would have never again had any confidence in preaching."

Imagine the outcome if this young man had decided the displeasure of his fellow passengers wasn't worth a dime's worth of honesty?

Our influence is like a shadow; it may fall even where we think we've never been. We also need to realize there are no "time-outs" or "vacations" we can take in keeping the Lord's commandments or being true to our consciences.

Stay on track with what you know is right!

Live to explain thy doctrine by thy life.

MATTHEW PRIOR

SOMEONE WHO UNDERSTANDS

Who, being in very nature God . . .
made himself nothing, taking the
very nature of a servant, being
made in human likeness.

PHILIPPIANS 2:6-7

One evening, a man refused to attend church with his wife. He was a good man but could not believe the story of God coming to earth as a man. So he stayed at home and waited for his family to return later.

Shortly after, snow began to fall heavily. A loud thud against his front door startled the man. When the sounds continued, he opened the front door to investigate. There he saw a flock of birds, huddled in the snow. In a desperate search for shelter, they had tried to fly through his large front window.

The man felt sorry for the birds and tried to direct them to a barn in the back of his house. He opened the barn doors and turned on a light. But the birds would not come. The man scattered bread crumbs on the snow, making a trail from the front door to the stable entrance. Still the birds ignored him. He tried catching them and then shooing at them. They only scattered.

Realizing the birds were frightened, he thought, If only I can think of some way to make them trust me. If only I could be a bird, talk with them, speak their language. Then I could show them the way—so they could really hear and see and understand.

About that time, the church bells began to ring. As he listened to the glad tidings, the truth dawned. The man sank to his knees in the snow.[48]

Just like those little frightened birds could only relate to another bird like themselves, God sent His Son, Jesus, to earth so that He could relate to us and we to Him. The next time your friends are hurt or lonely and in need of someone to talk to, let them know that there is someone who truly hears and sees and understands where they are and what they're going through.

That someone is Jesus.

I never ask the wounded person how he feels; I myself become the wounded person.

WALT WHITMAN

A PERMANENT COMPANION

What little girl wouldn't love to have a new doll? One that eats, wets, talks, walks—or one that is nothing but a silent bedtime companion. Every year the toy shelves burst with new models, just waiting to be dubbed the child's favorite doll.

Author Dale Galloway shares a story by R. E. Thomas that makes us rethink just what constitutes a "favorite" among some children:

"Do you like dollies?" the little girl asked her house guest.

"Yes, very much," the man responded.

"Then I'll show you mine," was the reply. Thereupon she presented one by one a whole family of dolls.

"And now tell me," the visitor asked, "which is your favorite doll?"

The child hesitated for a moment and then she said, "You're quite sure you like dollies, and will you please promise not to smile if I show you my favorite?" The man solemnly promised, and the girl hurried from the room. In a moment she returned with a tattered and dilapidated old doll. Its hair had come off; its nose was broken; its cheeks were scratched; an arm and leg were missing.

"Well, well," said the visitor, "and why do you like this one best?"

"I love her most," said the little girl, "because if I didn't love her, no one else would."[49]

God knows our condition: tattered lives, broken hearts, blind eyes, missing parts. If He didn't love us, no one else would. That's why He sent Jesus as a permanent companion for us—anytime, day or night.

God is in all things and in every place. There is not a place in the world in which he is not most truly present. Just as birds, wherever they fly, always meet with the air, so we, wherever we go, or wherever we are, always find God present.

SAINT FRANCIS OF SALES

FESTIVAL OF LIGHTS

The menorah, a candelabra with four candles on each side and one in the middle, actually represents a miracle. It is used during the winter Jewish holiday known as Hanukkah, or the Festival of Lights.

Hanukkah, which means dedication, commemorates the revolt against the Syrian Greeks in 167-164 BC, when the Jews recaptured the temple and rededicated it to God's service.

"Let your light shine before men in such a way that they may see your good works, and glorify your Father who is in heaven."

MATTHEW 5:16 NASB

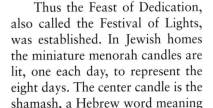

The Greeks had extinguished the great seven-branched candelabra in the temple, and only enough oil remained for the light to burn one day. It took eight days for the priests to consecrate more oil. Nevertheless, the Jews lit the lampstand, and it continued to burn for eight full days!

Thus the Feast of Dedication, also called the Festival of Lights, was established. In Jewish homes the miniature menorah candles are lit, one each day, to represent the eight days. The center candle is the shamash, a Hebrew word meaning servant, and it is used to light the other candles. From Scripture, Christians know that Jesus is the Light of the World, God's shamash.[50]

The Jerusalem temple has been destroyed, but when we receive Christ, we become the temple of God and the shamash shines in our hearts. We become lights in a dark world. Through His Holy Spirit we have a never-ending supply of oil to keep our lamps brightly burning.

I don't have to light all the world,
but I do have to light my part.

ANONYMOUS

A Change of Direction

The shepherds went back,
glorifying and praising God
for all that they had heard and
seen, just as had been told them.

Luke 2:20 NASB

Kenda's family, while on vacation, rented a car to drive on the backroads of beautiful British Columbia. He parents sat in the front; and she and her sisters, Kaylyn and Kyleigh sat in the back.

Her father was driving along when they saw a dirt road angling to the right with the correct highway number posted. Her mother said, "Surely that isn't the main road. Maybe the sign was turned. Look, the road straight ahead is paved and lined with utility poles too."

After a lighthearted discussion, the family took a vote and decided to stay on what appeared to be the main highway. After a few miles, the girls' father drove up a little hill, and then suddenly all they could see was water, a few small buildings, and a campground sign. The road came to a dead end there at a lovely lake and campsite. The family began laughing as Dad wheeled the car around and headed back to the dirt road turn they had passed. Eventually, the humble highway meandered into the most magnificent scenery of all.

We could easily stay on the broad, paved road and mindlessly travel to the dead end. Or we could change our thinking and our plans, turn down the narrow road to the Cross, and worship the King. Which will you choose?

The crossroads are down here:
which way to pull the rein?
The left brings you but loss,
the right nothing but gain.

ANGELUS SILESIUS

A GIFT OF LOVE

Kids made fun of "old woman Smith."

"Everyone knows she's crazy!" they said.

"She's not crazy," Tessie defended repeatedly. "Maybe she doesn't have any family. Maybe she's just lonely."

"But she claims people try to steal her money."

"She's poor like us. Just look at her run-down house and the filth in her yard."

"And she's grumpier than my bulldog!"

But Tessie ignored their taunts and adopted Mrs. Smith as her own special project. All through the year, she picked up trash and pulled her neighbor's weeds. In spring she planted flowers in her yard. She ran errands for the old woman and visited her daily.

> "Give, and it will be given to you. A good measure, pressed down, shaken together and running over, will be poured into your lap."
>
> LUKE 6:38

Never once did Mrs. Smith say "thank you." And no one else seemed to care. Only once did Tessie see a stranger, a middle-aged man, enter the widow's house.

One evening, Tessie took Mrs. Smith a basket of fruit and a special handmade gift. When no one answered the door, Tessie cautiously peered in, calling out her name softly.

Inside on the living room couch lay Mrs. Smith. She apparently had died in her sleep. In her lap was a small, unwrapped gift.

Tessie, her mom, and one man attended the woman's funeral—the same man Tessie had seen at Mrs. Smith's house a few weeks earlier.

The man handed Tessie the box she had seen in the old woman's lap. "I'm Mrs. Smith's lawyer," he said.

Tessie opened up the box, and inside was a cashier's check to her for $100,000, along with a note: "For college education first. Then spend wisely—as you wish."

Henry Wadsworth Longfellow said, "Give what you have. To someone it may be better than you dare to think." Giving out of love may not make us wealthy, but the return investment will be more than we give away—always.

> He who bestows his goods
> upon the poor, Shall have as
> much again, and ten times more.
>
> JOHN BUNYAN

Uproot the Tree

After months of searching, a lawyer and his family bought a house. They loved everything about it, especially the shady backyard. The contract went well—until the inspector finished his examination of the foundation.

"You have a tree growing too close to the house," he said. "If you don't remove it, the roots will eventually erode the foundation and cause it to shift. First, you'll see cracks on the inside walls, and then a major break on the outside brick structure. If you uproot the tree now and start watering the foundation regularly, the problem will correct itself—a minor cost of five hundred dollars for tree removal.

The lawyer's wife grew angry. "The reason we wanted this house was because of the trees, especially that one! We'll take our chances!"

"There is . . . a time to plant and a time to uproot."

ECCLESIASTES 3:1-2

So they moved in. They planted an expensive garden underneath the tree and enjoyed the shade all year long. One day, the lawyer noticed large cracks on the inside walls, and a jagged line followed the two-inch split in the outside brick wall—only a few feet from the tree roots.

The disgusted lawyer listed the house for sale immediately, but no one would buy the home. Finally, two years later, a realtor found a buyer with one condition: the owners repair the house before the sale.

By this time, the foundation needed a complete restoration. The cost? Just over ten thousand dollars. Eager to move out, the lawyer paid the money and sold the house at a substantial loss.

Like the lawyer's shade tree, little problems in life often appear harmless. If we ignore God's warnings to pull them up by the roots, those problems will eventually grow large enough to erode our spiritual foundation. We can avoid needless costly mistakes by listening—and heeding—God's words.

One's first step in wisdom is to question everything. And one's last is to come to terms with everything.

GEORG CHRISTOPH LICHTENBERG

The Twelve Days
of Giving

"Freely you have received, freely give."

MATTHEW 10:8

Patricia Moss listened to her children whine and cry in the toy department over which toy they'd get at Christmas and watched the pushing and shoving of the department store crowds. Then she stepped back for a minute to examine her family's values.

She decided to adopt a friend's tradition originating from the song, "The Twelve Days of Christmas." Beginning early in fall, she would try to pick a family that might need encouragement to get into the Christmas spirit. Then twelve days before Christmas, she and her family would begin slipping anonymous gifts onto the front porch of that family. They would write cute poems to go with the gifts, such as, "Twelve days before Christmas, a true friend gave to me, twelve candy canes, to hang upon the tree." The eleventh day before Christmas might be eleven fancy bows, the tenth day, a tin of ten giant homemade cookies, on and on right up to Christmas Day.

One year the Moss family chose an elderly man who had suffered a stroke. He and his wife had decided not to put up a tree that year until the "twelve days" gifts started arriving. Another year they selected two families to cheer because both sons had friends whose families needed their love and care.

Patricia said that even after her sons were grown and had moved away, they still participated in this tradition when they returned home for Christmas.[51]

Patricia taught her children well, allowing them a hands-on opportunity not only to see good, but also to do good, moving them beyond their own problems as they gave generously of themselves to others.

Every gift which is given, even though it be small, is great if given with affection.

PINDAR

Nowhere to Hide

"**H**ow did you know I was here?" Patty rested her head against the steel post of the bridge and swung her legs gently over the water below.

"Where else would you be?" her father, asked. He stood behind her, respecting her need for space. "This is where you always come when your heart hurts. After all these years, you don't think I know that?"

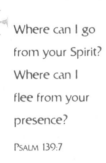

Where can I go from your Spirit? Where can I flee from your presence?

PSALM 139:7

Patty beckoned him to sit beside her. "In a way, I'm glad you know." He sat down. "I come out here to be alone, but I don't really want to be alone. Part of me needed you to know . . . to search and find me. I wanted to know that someone cared enough to worry about how I was doing." She paused. "I guess that's silly, huh?"

Her father took her hand in his. "No, it's not silly." He said nothing else. He just sat there, quietly supporting and loving her, knowing she needed to be alone but not alone, separate but still loved.

Our Heavenly Father knows us even more intimately than our own parents. When we try to run and hide from God's presence, He is always there—not as an intruder or accusing presence, but as a loving companion. He is a friend who holds us even when we're afraid to look Him in the eye. His love knows no hiding place. There is nothing to run from if we belong to Him. So often He won't speak a word when we try to escape Him. He just waits, acknowledging our choices and loving us just the same.

Have you run away from your Father? He is there if you want to talk to Him. He knows your heart, and He wants to be with you. Even in the moments of aloneness, God is your silent companion.

Though God be everywhere present, yet he is present to you in the deepest and most central part of the soul

WILLIAM LAW

MODERN MAGI

Some might think Rebecca Borkovec could easily play a child's version of the wife in the beloved Christmas story The Gift of the Magi. This eight-year-old third grader of Grendale, Wisconsin, heard aboutu the Locks of Love organization on a television commercial and decided to let her hair hang down for love—and a wig charity.

For two-and-a-half years Rebecca grew long, beautiful locks. At times, her hair was a real drag—literally. When she was swimming or shampooing, her hair would pull her head down in the water. Gymnastics brought problems too. Drying time seemed endless. But Rebecca kept her goal in sight. One day her hair would make a wonderful Christmas present for a child who had lost hair during chemotherapy. Rebecca's mother encouraged her, took time to braid her hair, and kept fixing it in creative ways. And Rebecca reminded her mom often, "We have to get it trimmed, so it will look nice for someone."

> Do not forget to do good and to share with others, for with such sacrifices God is pleased.
>
> HEBREWS 13:16

On February 9, 2000, Rebecca settled into a chair at Barbaba's TLC hair salon and signaled Barbara to start cutting. Was Rebecca sad to see her locks fall? She just sat there smiling. Why? "Because then the next time I went into the water, my head wouldn't be drooping down, and I was smiling because I was going to help people."

But Rebecca didn't stop there. "I'm going to do it again," she promised, "so I can help them again." It will probably take about three years.[52]

Most people give, if their money is headed toward research or a tax write-off and if the sacrifice is not too great or time-consuming. Rebecca's gift brought her no tangible returns, only the sheer joy of knowing she gave a headful of love to someone in need.

True charity is the desire to be useful to others without thought of recompense.

EMANUEL SWEDENBORG

DO ALL THE
GOOD YOU CAN

"Love your enemies,
do good to them."

LUKE 6:35

Years ago, some townspeople wanted to share God's love in a practical way. They planted a vegetable garden beside the railroad tracks in a deserted area outside of town. The townspeople hoed, planted, and watered the garden until it produced a great harvest.

With knowing smiles, they laid down their tools in the garden and went about their business, content to let nature take its course.

Over the next year, they planted nothing else and never picked a vegetable. But the garden grew and grew, yet vegetables seldom rotted in the garden. Weeds were scarce, and the garden always seemed to have that "specially tended to" look.

Was it a miracle? Perhaps. An untold number of homeless hobos riding the railroads—perhaps hundreds—

helped themselves to the crop and often spent many hours looking after the garden.

The hobos could always count on the blessings of good food—especially tasty as the fruit of their hard labors.

All around us are "hungry hobos" who need to know someone cares. Look for practical ways to share the love of Jesus with anyone who needs Him. You may be surprised by the harvest you reap.

Charity sees the need,

not the cause.

GERMAN PROVERB

MISPLACED EXPECTATIONS

Most of us at some time indulge in the endless chase for perfection: perfect body, just-right hair, lots of friends, no conflicts. And most of us discover quickly the futility of such expectations.

Every year Dear Abby prints a familiar story written by Emily Kingsley called, "Welcome to Holland." Emily, a writer, lecturer, and talented mother of an adult child with Downs syndrome, knows about expectations. Others have asked her what it's like raising a child with disabilities. In her story, Emily uses a metaphor. She compares the expectation of a child's birth to planning a vacation trip to Italy. She mentions the joy of deciding on tourist spots to visit and the anticipation of all the sights you would see upon your arrival.

Give thanks in all circumstances, for this is God's will for you in Christ Jesus.

I THESSALONIANS 5:18

She then describes the scenario upon landing in your vacation spot. Surely a mistake has been made, because the stewardess on your plane welcomes you not to Italy, but to Holland. You argue, but nothing changes. You are in Holland, and there you will stay.

Anyone who has ever been to Holland knows that tulips, windmills, and Rembrandts make Holland a beautiful place as well. Emily points out that it's just not what you expected. You planned on going to Italy.

In her poignant illustration, Kingsley challenges the reader to focus not on unmet expectations (Italy), but on the beauty of where you are (Holland).

When life doesn't turn out perfectly—the way we planned—we have a choice. Whether it's as minor as a holiday gone awry or as major as a Prince Charming that turned into an ugly frog, God wants us to celebrate that "very special, very lovely thing" about our circumstance. Keep looking. You'll find it.

Good when he gives,
supremely good,
Nor less when he denies,
E'en crosses from his sovereign hand
Are blessings in disguise.

JAMES HERVEY

Good News

Christmas letters. They come every December if the author is well prepared. Some don't arrive until late January. Those come from the harried and hurried whose lives were just too complicated in late fall to do anything different. But whenever they arrive, they are welcome.

They may be tucked into a greeting card or accompanied by a snapshot. They may come all alone, in their own envelope, bearing their own cancelled stamp. They may be handwritten, computer processed, or churned out by a copying machine. But however they are delivered, they are treasured.

Some fill only one sheet; others ramble on for pages. Some are candid and humorous; others bring concerns and sadness. But all are filled with a common element. All bring news from far away.

Good news from far away is like cold water to the thirsty.

Proverbs 25:25 TLB

Christmas letters. We've all come to expect them each year. That letter may be the only opportunity we have to reconnect with acquaintances and catch up on their family's happenings.

But Christmas letters can be more than newsletters about friends' activities. One recipient takes the

Christmas letters she receives and divides them into four piles, setting one pile aside for each quarter of the year. During that three-month period, she prays for the authors of those letters and, as time permits, even pens a quick note to say "hello." In this way, the Christmas letters she receives each year bring her good news but also bring the sender her thoughts and prayers. Her simple gesture creates a refreshing circle of love.

What will you do with your Christmas letters this year?

Life is the flower of which love is the honey.

VICTOR HUGO

References

Unless otherwise indicated, all Scripture quotations are taken from the Holy Bible, New International Version® NIV®. Copyright © 1973, 1978, 1984 by International Bible Society. Used by permission of Zondervan Publishing House. All rights reserved.

Scripture quotations marked NKJV are taken from The New King James Version. Copyright © 1979, 1980, 1982, Thomas Nelson, Inc.

Scripture quotations marked KJV are taken from the King James Version of the Bible.

Scripture quotations marked NASB are taken from the New American Standard Bible. Copyright © The Lockman Foundation 1960, 1962, 1963, 1968, 1971, 1972, 1973, 1975, 1977, 1995. Used by permission.

Scripture quotations marked AMP are taken from The Amplified Bible. Old Testament copyright © 1965, 1987 by Zondervan Corporation, Grand Rapids Michigan. New Testament copyright © 1958, 1987 by The Lockman Foundation, La Habra, California. Used by permission.

Scripture quotations marked RSV are taken from the Revised Standard Version. Coyright © 1946, 1952, Division of Christian Education of the National Council of the Churches of Christ.

Scripture quotations marked ASV are taken from the American Standard Version. Copyright © 1901 by Thomas Nelson & Sons and copyright © 1929 by International Council of Religious Education.

Scripture quotations marked CEV are taken from the Contemporary English Version, copyright © 1991, 1992, 1995 by American Bible Society. Used by permission.

Scripture quotations marked NRSV are from the New Revised Standard Version of the Bible, copyright © 1989 by The Division of Christian Edcation of the National Council of the Churches of Christ in the USA. Used by permission. All rights reserved.

Verses marked TLB are taken from The Living Bible © 1971. Used by permission of Tyndale House Publishers, Inc., Wheaton, Illinois 60189. All rights reserved.

Endnotes

1 Illustrations for Preaching and Teaching, Craig B. Larson (Grand Rapids, MI: Baker Book House, 1993), p. 122.

2 Knight's Master Book of 4,000 Illustrations, Walter B. Knight (Grand Rapids, MI: William B. Erdmans Publishing Co., 1956), p. 64.

3 Ibid, p. 71.

4 Macartney's Illustrations, Clarence E. Macartney (NY: Abingdon Press, 1945, 1946), pp. 19, 172.

5 A Guide to Prayer for All God's People, Rueben P. Job and Norman Shawchuck, ed. (Nashville: Upper Room Books, 1990), pp. 326-328.

6 The Diary of a Young Girl, Anne Frank, (New York, NY: Doubleday, 1952).

7 Ibid.

8 Marilyn Elias, "Volunteer Pilots Wing Patients to Hospitals," USA Today, June 10, 1996, p. 04D.

9 Today in the Word, February 1991, p. 10.

10 Today in the Word, September 2, 1992.

11 Maya Angelou, Wouldn't Take Nothin' for My Journey Now, New York, Random House, 1993, p. 62.

12 Today in the Word, Moody Bible Institute, January 1992, p. 8.

13 Author Unknown

14 Meryle Secrest, Leonard Bernstein: A Life, Knopf, 1995.

15 Common Ground, January 1990.

16 "Ansel Adams," Morning Edition, November 24, 1997 (National Public Radio).

17 Maugham, W. Somerset, Of Human Bondage, Doubleday, Garden City, New York, 1936.

[18] Chorus by Mary Maxwell, Score by Ada Rose Gibbs.

[19] Today in the Word May 1990, MBI.

[20] Nanette Thorsen-Snipes. Adapted from Power for Living, April 1992.

[21] The Finishing Touch, Charles Swindoll (Dallas: Word Publishing, 1994), p. 274.

[22] Spiritual Disciplines for the Christian Life, Donald S. Whitney (Colorado Springs: NavPress, 1991), p. 37.

[23] Reader's Digest, October 1991, p. 59-62.

[24] Illustrations Unlimited James Hewett, ed. (Wheaton: Tyndale House, 1988), p. 159.

[25] Gary Johnson, Reader's Digest, September 1991, p. 164-165.

[26] The Finishing Touch, Charles R. Swindoll (Dallas: Word Publishing, 1994), pp. 186-187.

[27] The Last Word, Jamie Buckingham (Plainfield, NJ: Logos International, 1978), p. 169-170.

[28] Decision, March 1996, p. 33.

[29] A Moment a Day, Mary Beckwith and Kathi Mills, ed., (Ventura, CA: Regal Books, 1988), p. 25.

[30] "Won by One," Ron Rand, The Inspirational Study Bible, Max Lucado, ed. (Dallas: Word, 1995), pp. 604-605.

[31] A Moment a Day, Mary Beckwith and Kathi Mills, ed. (Ventura, CA: Regal Books, 1988), p. 247.

[32] Encyclopedia of 7700 Illustrations, Paul Lee Tan (Garland, TX: Bible Communications Inc., 1979), p. 1387.

[33] Give Your Life a Lift, Herman W. Gockel (St. Louis: Concordia Publishing House, 1968), p. 38-39.

[34] People, March 18, 1996, p. 62.

[35] San Luis Obispo Telegram/Tribune, March 9, 1996, p. E4.

[36] Encyclopedia of 7700 Illustrations, Paul Lee Tan (Garland, TX: Bible Communications Inc., 1979), pp. 1477-1479.

37 Artists Who Created Great Works, Cathie Cush. (Austin, TX: Raintree Steck-Vaughn Company, 1995), pp. 24-25.

38 Carlsbad Caverns Silent Chambers, Timeless Beauty, John Barnett. (Carlsbad, NM: Carlsbad Caverns-Guadalupe Mountains Association, 1981), p. 2.

39 A Young Patriot: The American Revolution as Experienced by One Boy, Jim Murphy (New York: Clarion Books, 1996), p. 47.

40 Adapted from The Upper Room, January-February, 1999. January 30, 1999.

41 Adapted from Daily Wisdom, January 26, 1999.

42 Wayne Rice. Adapted Daily Wisdom, January 25, 1999. Edited from Youth Talks, Youth Specialties, 1994.

43 Kelly McHugh. Adapted from The Upper Room, January-February, 1999. January 9, 1999.

44 Sequoia & Kings Canyon: The Story Behind the Scenery, William C. Tweed. (Las Vegas, NV: KC Publications, 1980), pp. 2-29.

45 He Cares, He Comforts, Corrie ten Boom. (Old Tappan, NJ: Fleming H. Revell, 1977), pp. 29-33.

46 Nanette Thorsen-Snipes, Southern Lifestyles, Summer 1996, p. 38.

47 Thomas J. Burns, "The Second Greatest Cristmas Story Ever," Reader's Digest (December 1989), pp. 10-11.

48 Author of story unknown.

49 Dale E. Galloway, You Can Win with Love (Irvine: Harvest House, 1976), pp. 24-25.

50 Steven Ger, "The Undying Flame," Kindred Spirit (Winter 1999), pp. 42-43.

51 Dallas Morning News (February 2, 1992).

52 Gary Rummier, "Girl, 8, Lets Down Her Hair for Wig Charity," Wichita Falls Times Record News (February 26, 2000), pp.138-139.

Additional copies of this book and
other teen titles from Honor Books
are available from your local bookstore.

Real Teens, Real Stories, Real Life

E-mail from God for Teens

WWJD Stories for Teens

God's Little Devotional Book for Teens

If you have enjoyed this book,
or if it has impacted your life,
we would like to hear from you. Please contact us at:

Honor Books
Department E
P.O. Box 55388
Tulsa, Oklahoma 74155

Or, by e-mail at info@honorbooks.com